PALMS, PASSION, & RESURRECTION

*Holy Week According to
Mark's Gospel*

A Lenten Study

ANDREW CURTIS LAY

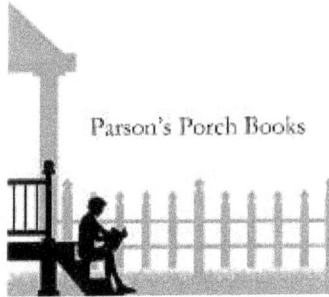

Parson's Porch Books

Palms, Passion, & Resurrection
ISBN: Softcover 978-1-960326-06-5
Copyright © 2023 by Andrew Curtis Lay

Parson's Porch Books is an imprint of Parson's Porch & Company (PP&C) in Cleveland, Tennessee. PP&C is a self-funded charity which earns money by publishing books of noted authors, representing all genres. Its face and voice is **David Russell Tullock** who you can contact at: dtullock@parsonsporch.com.

Parson's Porch & Company *turns books into bread & milk* by sharing its profits with the poor.

www.parsonsporch.com

PALMS, PASSION, & RESURRECTION

Holy Week According to Mark's Gospel

The practice of resurrection is an intentional, deliberate decision to believe and participate in resurrection life, life out of death, life that trumps death, life that is the last word, Jesus' life.

- Eugene Peterson

Left to ourselves we lapse into a kind of collusion with entropy, acquiescing in the general belief that things may be getting worse but that there's nothing much we can do about them. And we are wrong. Our task in the present... is to live as resurrection people in between Easter and the final day, with our Christian life, corporate and individual, in both worship and mission, as a sign of the first and a foretaste of the second.

- N.T. Wright

To Ally and Jane, my world.

ACKNOWLEDGEMENTS

First and foremost, I want to thank my wife, Ally, for her continued love and support. She has encouraged me to put myself out there and write this book. She is the most caring, kind, and compassionate human being that I know. I'm thankful to have her by my side as my life partner. She is a wonderful wife and an incredible mother to our daughter.

I am grateful to my parents who are always supportive and encouraging. They taught me to work hard at everything I do. I'm so thankful for the ways that they have loved and supported me throughout my life.

I want to thank my entire family for their continued love and encouragement as well. What a joy it is to have them as my family and to have them all in my life.

I want to share my appreciation for my friends. I am so thankful for their friendship and comradery. I am so lucky to have such a great group of companions to share in life's greatest moments with. Thank you all for your friendship.

I want to thank all the folks at Parson's Porch & Company who helped, supported, and encouraged me throughout this process. I am especially grateful to David Russell Tullock, the publisher, who stayed in contact with me and guided this process

Finally, I am grateful to all the folks at Wesley Memorial and Carlock United Methodist Churches for their support and encouragement. It is a blessing to share in ministry with them as their pastor.

Andrew Curtis Lay

CONTENTS

The Palm Branch – a symbol of victory, triumph, peace, and eternal life.

The Passion – comes from the Latin word *passionem* which means suffering or enduring.

The Resurrection – the rising again to life; resurgence; revival.

THE JERUSALEM TEMPLE

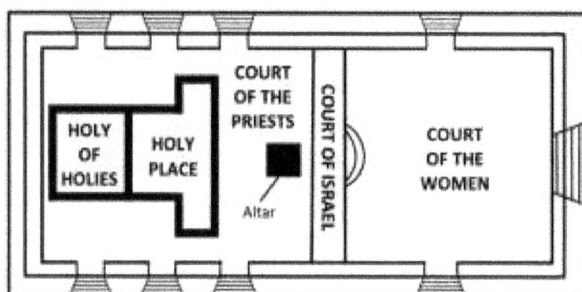

HOLY OF HOLIES · HOLY PLACE · COURT OF THE PRIESTS · COURT OF ISRAEL · COURT OF THE WOMEN · Altar · COURT OF THE GENTILES

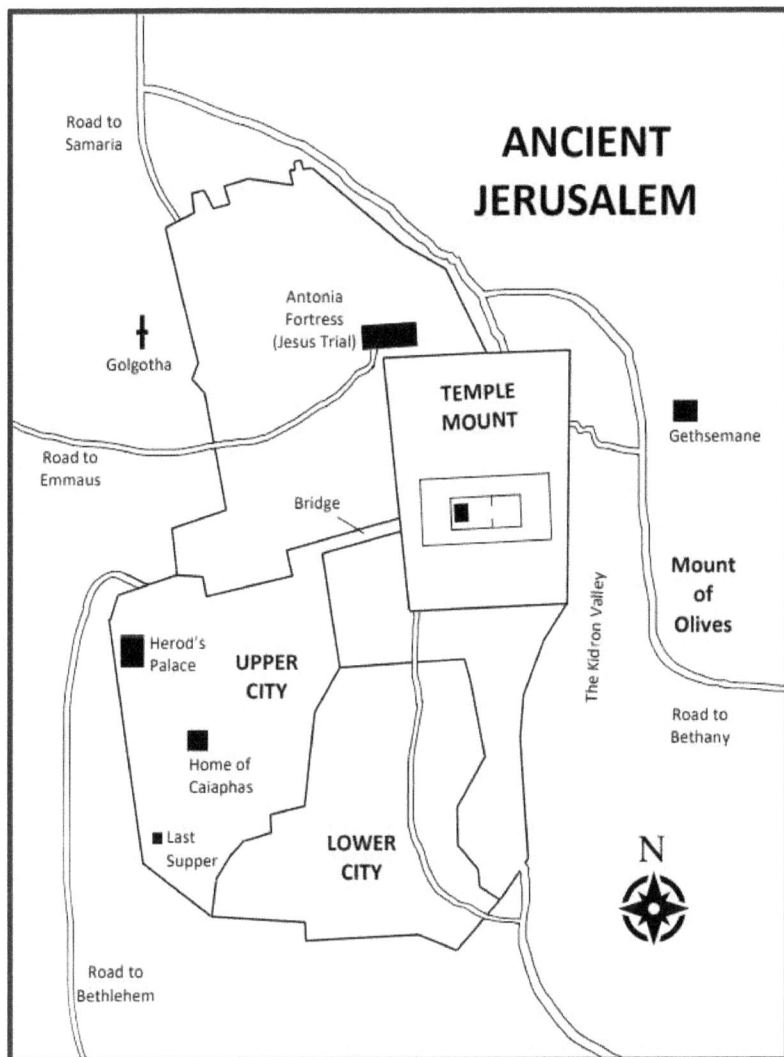

ANCIENT JERUSALEM

Road to Samaria

Antonia Fortress (Jesus Trial)

Golgotha

TEMPLE MOUNT

Gethsemane

Road to Emmaus

Bridge

Mount of Olives

The Kidron Valley

Herod's Palace

UPPER CITY

Road to Bethany

Home of Caiaphas

Last Supper

LOWER CITY

N

Road to Bethlehem

INTRODUCTION

I was in my junior year of high school when my Sunday school class at church decided that we would all collectively give up chocolate for Lent.

Hardly two days had passed before I broke that pact. I was over at my friend Aaron's house when he offered me a Klondike bar.

I typically don't eat a lot of sweets and desserts, but for some reason I accepted the offer. I suppose even I couldn't say no to a hunk of vanilla ice cream covered in a thin chocolatey shell. I had just finished the last bite when I remembered the promise that I had made to my Sunday school class.

In a panic I shouted, "Oh my gosh, I forgot I gave up chocolate for Lent!"

To which Aaron cleverly replied, "What would Andrew do for a Klondike bar? ... He would break Lent."

Lent is a season of forty days, excluding Sundays, that begins on Ash Wednesday and helps us prepare for the coming of Easter. During Lent, we recall when Jesus went out into the wilderness, fasted for forty days, and was tempted by Satan as he prepared for the beginning of his earthly ministry. As the Gospel of Mark states:

> *And the Spirit immediately drove him out into the wilderness. He was in the wilderness forty days, tempted by Satan; and he was with the wild beasts; and the angels waited on him.*
>
> *(Mark 1:12, 13)*[1]

Like Jesus's time in the wilderness, we too are invited into a season of fasting as we examine the condition of our spirits. Traditionally, Christians around the world participate in the season of Lent by giving something up (like chocolate) in order the share in the sacrifice of Jesus Christ. Lent is also an opportunity to add something (like prayer and study) to grow closer to Christ in preparation for Easter.

Lent is a time that is ripe for repentance, prayer, fasting, and almsgiving. It is a time of purification, repentance, and redemption. It is a time of self-sacrifice and discipline as we confront our sin, confess our guilt, and seek repentance for our lives.

The season of Lent is crucial to our Christian development because it invites us to look inward and ask essential questions of self-introspection, like: What is in my life, that should no longer be in my life? What do I need to change? What steps do I need to take to better follow Jesus? How might I become holy as God is holy?

As we navigate these questions, we are invited to reflect on the condition of our hearts. In our exploration we can realize our need for God's divine grace in our own lives and find assurance that we have indeed been forgiven.

This book *Palms, Passion, and Resurrection: Holy Week According to Mark's Gospel,* is designed to be a devotional resource for those seeking a deeper connection to God in the Lenten season. In each chapter, we journey with Jesus through the events of Holy Week according to the Gospel of Mark.

There are many reasons for using the Gospel of Mark as the primary source for this study. It is the earliest and shortest of the four Gospels and is believed to be a source used by both

Matthew and Luke. Mark's Gospel is set apart due to its portrayal of Christ as a suffering servant. Furthermore, the crucifixion is described in bloody and brutal detail.[2]

Mark's Gospel moves rapidly, but then slows down during the Passion narrative, devoting six chapters to the last week of Jesus. Mark's account also chronicles Jesus' last week in the greatest detail, giving a day-by-day account.

As we walk alongside Jesus during Holy Week, we bear witness to the passion story. We join the crowd's praises during Jesus' triumphal entry into Jerusalem on Palm Sunday. We witness Jesus cleansing the Temple, overturning the tables, and driving out the money changers. We listen to Jesus' teachings in the Temple as he addresses some of the religious leader's questions. We smell the oil that is poured on Jesus' head during his anointing. We sit with Jesus at the table, alongside the disciples, in the Upper Room during the Last Supper. We pray with Jesus as he agonizes in the Garden of Gethsemane where he is betrayed and arrested. We watch helplessly during Jesus' trial, crucifixion, and death on the cross. Ultimately, we celebrate Jesus' victory over death through the resurrection.

In this book, we experience the palm, the passion, and the resurrection. The palm branch is a symbol of victory, triumph, peace, and eternal life. The passion comes from the Latin word *passionem* which means "suffering or enduring." The resurrection comes from the Latin term *resurgere* which means "the rising again to life; resurgence; revival." The palm, passion, and the resurrection are intertwined in a paradox portraying Jesus' mortal humanity and his divine triumph over death.

Throughout the story of Holy Week, we see Jesus celebrated and praised as the Messiah, the king who has come to bring redemption and peace. On the flip side, we also see Jesus at his most vulnerable, hanging on the cross. The crowds shout, "Hosanna," but they also shout, "Crucify him!" The palms, passion, and resurrection are all present and at the forefront in Jesus' final week.

Together, we journey with Jesus as we follow him from palm to passion and finally to resurrection. Ultimately, this journey leads us to the celebration of the empty tomb. In this celebration we experience God's redemption in a meaningful and life-giving way.

My hope is that, during the season of Lent, you will encounter the story of Jesus' resurrection in a fresh and exciting new way. May you be filled with God's redemption and grace as we embark upon a Lenten journey through Jesus' final week in Jerusalem, leading up to the cross and the empty tomb, from palm, to passion, to resurrection.

Rev. Andrew Curtis Lay

CHAPTER ONE

JESUS ENTERS JERUSALEM

When they were approaching Jerusalem, at Bethphage and Bethany, near the Mount of Olives, he sent two of his disciples and said to them, "Go into the village ahead of you, and immediately as you enter it, you will find tied there a colt that has never been ridden; untie it and bring it. If anyone says to you, 'Why are you doing this?' just say this, 'The Lord needs it and will send it back here immediately.'" They went away and found a colt tied near a door, outside in the street. As they were untying it, some of the bystanders said to them, "What are you doing, untying the colt?" They told them what Jesus had said; and they allowed them to take it. Then they brought the colt to Jesus and threw their cloaks on it; and he sat on it. Many people spread their cloaks on the road, and others spread leafy branches that they had cut in the fields. Then those who went ahead and those who followed were shouting,

"Hosanna!
Blessed is the one who comes
in the name of the Lord!
Blessed is the coming kingdom
of our ancestor David!
Hosanna in the highest heaven!"

Then he entered Jerusalem and went into the temple; and when he had looked around at everything, as it was already late, he went out to Bethany with the twelve.

(Mark 11:1-11)

One of my favorite traditions in the Christian church is the practice of waving palm branches on Palm (or Passion) Sunday. Palm Sunday is an important day that marks the beginning of Holy Week, the week leading up to Easter. The church considers this to be the most sacred week in the Christian calendar.

During Holy Week we are invited to relive Jesus' final week in Jerusalem. We recall Jesus' entry into the city. We remember the journey that takes place from the waving of the palm branches to his nailing on the cross, resulting in his death. Ultimately, this timeline culminates in the celebration of Jesus' Resurrection on Easter Sunday.

Palm Sunday, which occurs exactly one week before Easter Sunday, is an especially festive day. Each year, on this day, churches around the world distribute palm branches to children and youth and invite them to parade around the sanctuary. The youngsters march around while waving their palm branches, shouting: "Hosanna in the highest! Blessed is he who comes in the name of the Lord!" (Mark 11:9).

I have fond childhood memories of waving palm branches in my home church at First United Methodist Church in Cleveland, Tennessee. I loved waving my palm branch in the air as the people from the congregation looked on and smiled with joy and pride. I can remember the feeling of importance that I experienced as I stomped down the aisles, waving my branch alongside the pews.

As a child, Palm Sunday was an especially exciting service, because I felt like I had an important role to play. I was able to actively offer my own praise to God in a very real and tangible way. For that reason, Palm Sunday was one of the highlights of the liturgical year for me growing up.

To those who might be unfamiliar with Palm Sunday, I can understand how this practice might seem unusual. If you didn't grow up in this tradition, it might seem strange to wave palm branches and march around the sanctuary during the middle of a church service.

The waving of palm branches, however, is an old tradition that marks the beginning of Jesus' final week before his crucifixion and resurrection. In this chapter, we will further explore the tradition of the palm branches as we recall Jesus' triumphal entry into Jerusalem when he came to celebrate the Passover festival.

The Passover Festival

For the Hebrew people, the Passover is the biggest celebration of the year. It is a week-long festival that commemorates the Exodus of the Israelites from Egyptian slavery. God had sent numerous plagues upon Pharoah and Egypt, because of Pharoah's refusal to free the Israelites from slavery.

In the last plague, Moses instructed the Israelites to follow God's command by placing sacrificial blood from a lamb on their doorposts. Then God sent the angel of death to the land of Egypt. The angel of death killed the first-born child from every house, but the angel passed over the homes that had placed the sacrificial blood on their doorposts. This is a huge moment in the history of the Hebrew people, because it marks God's covenant with God's chosen people.

Therefore, the Exodus of God's people in Egypt became an important festival that was celebrated every year and became known as the Passover. According to the Old Testament, it was required for all Jewish males to travel to Jerusalem at least once in their lifetime to celebrate one of the special Hebrew festivals. The Law states:

> *Three times a year all your males shall appear before the Lord your God at the place that he will choose: at the festival of unleavened bread, at the festival of weeks, and at the festival of booths. They shall not appear before the Lord empty-handed; all shall give as they are able, according to the blessing of the Lord your God that he has given you.*
>
> *(Deuteronomy 16:16, 17)*

Some of the most devout Jewish people would make this pilgrimage every single year, but many would come once every few years. Still, some would come only even once in a lifetime.

Not only did people of the Jewish faith go to Jerusalem, but travelers from all over the surrounding area would go to celebrate in the Holy City. During the Passover, the city of Jerusalem was a bustling metropolis full of celebration and festivity.

The Jewish historian Josephus, a contemporary of the Gospel writers, indicates that during the Passover celebration, the population of Jerusalem increased to more than two million people![3] That is a massive amount of people considering the normal population of Jerusalem during that time was around approximately 40,000 people.

According to the Passion narrative, Jesus is among these pilgrims who were traveling to the Holy City to celebrate the Passover festival. This was not the first time Jesus has done this. In fact, Jesus had made this journey before.

In the Gospel of Luke, we see Jesus accompany Joseph and Mary when he was a 12-year-old boy (Luke 2:41-52). John's Gospel refers to Jesus traveling to Jerusalem a few other times to celebrate the Passover festival (see John 2:13; 6:4; 12:12).

Jesus has traveled to Jerusalem for the Passover before, and here Jesus returns for this celebration. In this pilgrimage, Jesus sets a series of events in motion and, as a result, things will never be the same again.

Grand Theft Burro

As Jesus approaches Jerusalem, from the east, he decides to throw a little parade for himself as he enters the Holy City. It appears that Jesus has a flair for the dramatic as he orchestrates this big event with the help of his disciples. Jesus tells two of his disciples to go into the village and get a donkey. Jesus says:

"Go into the village ahead of you, and immediately as you enter it, you will find tied there a colt that has never been ridden; untie it and bring it. If anyone says to you, 'Why are you doing this?' just say this, 'The Lord needs it and will send it back here immediately.'"

(Mark 11:2, 3)

The theologian Tom Long suggests that perhaps the two disciples who were put on "donkey detail" were James and John. Long points out that it would have been ironic of Jesus to pick these two brothers because, only hours before, James and John had asked Jesus to grant them places of honor, one on his right and one on his left, when Jesus goes to be seated in glory.[4]

James and John are completely preoccupied with their own status in life. Jesus, astounded by their request, is quick to let them know that they are completely missing the point.

If we are being honest with ourselves, we fall into this trap as well. We argue, we fight, and we compare ourselves to one another. We think we deserve special treatment, and we think that we are sometimes better than the people around us. We fall into the trap of entitlement. We think we deserve certain things and have the right to do what we want.

What would Jesus think about our arguments? What would Jesus think about our quest for greatness? What would Jesus think about our practice of elevating ourselves and demoting our neighbors? What would Jesus think about the way we treat the least, the lost, and the lonely?

Surprisingly, Jesus does not chastise James and John. He does not yell at them, shame them, or guilt them. Instead, Jesus uses this as a teaching moment and talks about the importance of serving others.

Jesus knows that these two disciples have been jockeying for power and glory. By sending them to fetch a young colt, perhaps Jesus was teaching James and John a lesson about humility.

Still, this request has always seemed a bit shady to me. Is Jesus telling his followers to steal someone's donkey? Is he asking them to commit "Grand Theft Burro?" This does not seem like the typical behavior we might expect from Jesus, the Son of God.

I suppose one could argue that this isn't stealing. It is more like borrowing, but it still seems out of character for Jesus and a little hard to believe. It is doubtful that Jesus would ask his disciples to just go steal a random donkey.

The Jewish New Testament scholar, Amy-Jill Levine, suggests that Jesus probably arranged for this ahead of time.[5] After all, Jesus had a lot of friends in Bethany. This is where his friends Mary, Martha, and Lazarus lived. Lazarus is a man whom Jesus raised from the dead. Mary, Martha, and Lazarus kind of owe Jesus a favor. It is entirely possible that Jesus borrowed this donkey from them, or maybe even from someone else he knew in the area.

Therefore, the disciples go and borrow this burro, and it happens just as Jesus said it would. Some bystanders see the two disciples untying a colt and demand to know what is going on. The disciples spout off exactly what Jesus told them to say, and they are allowed to take the donkey.

Perhaps the most interesting thing about this encounter is that Jesus makes this request in this first place. After all, he has traveled almost the whole way to Jerusalem. Why would he want to ride in on a donkey now that he has almost arrived? This is something that you do at the beginning of a journey, not at the end. At this point, it seems like more of a hassle to go and get this donkey, bring it back, and saddle it up.

Furthermore, if you are going to make a grand entrance, then why would you ride in on a donkey? Why wouldn't you ride in on a horse? Why wouldn't you ride in on a stallion or a mustang? Why wouldn't you descend upon the crowd in a golden chariot pulled by a trusty steed? The difference between a donkey and a mustang is like the difference between a Go-cart and a Ferrari!

But Jesus is adamant about his decision to ride in on a donkey. Interestingly, this the only time we see Jesus riding a donkey throughout all the Gospels. Every time we see Jesus traveling around, he is either in a boat or on foot, walking. He never appears to travel by donkey, horse, car, or train. During this journey into Jerusalem, however, Jesus makes the intentional decision to ride upon a donkey, and he channels inspiration from the Old Testament.

King David's Donkey

Throughout the Old Testament, the act of riding of a donkey is viewed as a sign of royalty. David, the King of Israel, rode upon a donkey (1 Kings 1:33). This makes sense considering donkeys are sturdier, stronger, and can go longer with less water than horses. Not only are donkeys stronger than horses, but they are also highly intelligent. Donkeys can traverse the rocky terrain throughout Palestine, going places horses simply can't. In other words, you can take a donkey "off-roading."

King David isn't the only one who rode a donkey in the Scriptures. Many other figures in the Bible rode donkeys as well. For example, Abraham and Moses both rode donkeys (Genesis 22:3 and Exodus 4:20). In the book of Judges, we see that the judges of Israel rode donkeys (Judges 12:13-15).

Jesus follows the example of all these other heroes of the faith when he chooses a humble donkey, a simple burro, as his mode of transportation. Jesus does this, in part, to fulfill the prophecies of the Old Testament. We see this prophecy being fulfilled in the words of the prophet Zechariah from 550 years before Jesus' time:

Rejoice greatly, O daughter Zion! Shout aloud, O daughter Jerusalem! Lo, your king comes to you; triumphant and victorious is he, humble and riding on a donkey, on a colt, the foal of a donkey.

(Zechariah 9:9)

It is quite possible that Jesus' disciples are familiar with these Scriptures. Perhaps this is why they don't question Jesus when he requests a donkey for his means of transportation. It is also quite possible that the crowd is familiar with these prophecies as well because we see them react to Jesus' entrance in a very special way. This action is deliberate, and the people recognize the connection that Jesus is making here.

Jesus travels down the Mount of Olives as his arrival is celebrated by his supporters. The crowd celebrates Jesus as he passes by them. Of course, by now, most people know about Jesus. He has been traveling around healing the blind, the lame, and the sick. He has been out cleansing lepers and casting out demons. He has fed thousands of people, and he has even brought the dead back to life.

According to Matthew's Gospel, there are a few people in the crowd who don't know about Jesus. They ask the people around them why there is so much commotion in the city. They essentially ask, "What's the big deal? Who is this guy?"

The people in city are quick to answer, "It's Jesus, the prophet from Nazareth in Galilee" (Matthew 21:10, 11).

Imagine the follow up questions and answers from the people in the crowd saying, "This is the guy who performed all these great miracles. This is the guy who healed my cousin. This is the guy who preached on the mountaintop. This is the guy who has come to free us from oppression."

Jesus has built up a reputation as a king of the oppressed and suffering. Jesus spent his time with a group of fishermen who had become his disciples. He communed with sinners and rubbed shoulders with tax collectors and prostitutes. Jesus' closest followers were not the elite, rich, or powerful. They were the marginalized, underprivileged, and poor. Jesus was a king of the oppressed and suffering.

The Triumphal Entry

Jesus comes on the road into Jerusalem, riding on a humble donkey, marching through this triumphal parade. The people rejoice, throw their tattered cloaks and leafy branches on the road, and sing his praises as Jesus makes his way through this crowd of onlookers. The people celebrate this very unusual king during this very unusual parade.

I once had the pleasure of marching in a very unusual parade. Every three or four years, my high school marching band would travel to London, England to march in the Lord Mayor's New Year's Day Parade.

When I was a freshman in high school, I had the opportunity to go and march in that parade. My sister, who was a senior, was in the color guard, and I played the trumpet in the marching band (I later made the switch to tuba).

I vividly remember playing, "Play That Funky Music White Boy" as I marched throughout the streets of London, turning the corner at Piccadilly and trekking down White Hall toward Downing Street. The crowds shouted and sang along as we played in the city streets. It was an invigorating experience.

The only problem was that we followed behind a group of Clydesdale horses. Of course, the horses did what horses do. The streets were littered with manure. We marched, dodging and swerving, trying not to step in the mess.

Later, when we were back in the United States, our band directors printed t-shirts that read, "Mind the Poo." This is a phrase that mimicked the signs in the subway in England, "Mind the Gap," which basically means, "Watch your step."

Considering this story, it is a good thing that there was only *one* donkey in Jesus' parade, and he was the one riding it! There is not a parade of Clydesdales leading the way, so there is no need for Jesus to "mind the gap" or "watch his step." Jesus is the star of the show as he marches in his own parade and makes his triumphal entry into Jerusalem. As he proceeds down the street, the crowd sings out praises to Jesus:

"Hosanna!
Blessed is the one who comes
in the name of the Lord!
Blessed is the coming kingdom
of our ancestor David!
Hosanna in the highest heaven!"

(Mark 21:9, 10)

In their praises, the crowd shouts out the word *Hosanna* which means "Deliver us now. Save us now!" The people are offering this greeting that is traditionally given to a king. They are crying out to Jesus like they would a Messiah. In this act of devotion, they are recognizing Jesus as the promised Savior who has come to right the wrongs of the people of Israel. In their proclamation, the people are quoting a Psalm from the Old Testament: "Blessed is the one who comes in the name of the Lord. We bless you from the house of the Lord" (Psalm 118:26).

Psalm 118 is specifically written as a greeting to welcome kings back to Jerusalem from war. It is a celebratory greeting reserved for a king. This Psalm also alludes to the promise of a Messiah who has come to deliver God's people.

This Psalm is recited every year during the Passover festival. Perhaps this is the crowd's way of asking Jesus to free them from the tyranny of Rome much like God freed the Israelites from slavery in Egypt.

The crowd receives Jesus as the Messiah and king. They see him as a descendant of David who is taking his rightful kingship and believe that Jesus is indeed the promised king who has come to bring about deliverance for the Hebrew people.

They believe that Jesus has come to deliver them from the Romans so that Israel will be an independent kingdom once again. They long for freedom, peace, and prosperity. Now, they see that Jesus is riding into Jerusalem on a donkey, fulfilling the words of the prophet. Could this be? Could Jesus be the promised king who has come to deliver God's people?

With their hearts full of hope, the crowd covers the road with palm branches and garments. They essentially roll out the red carpet for Jesus. Only John's Gospel mentions that the crowd waves the palm branches in the air to greet Jesus and welcome him as their powerful new king.

Waves of Warning

I wish we could just end the story here and say, "Jesus lived happily ever after." I wish we could conclude this narrative right here and right now, because things take such a dark turn from this point forward. Just five days later, Jesus will face a crowd, but this time they won't be shouting "Hosanna." Instead, they will be shouting "Crucify Him!"

William H. Willimon, a retired bishop in the United Methodist Church, talks about how the waving of the palm branches might also be seen as an omen. He writes:

The waving of palm branches is usually interpreted as a biblical sign of welcome and hospitality. But one anthropologist notes that, in some cultures, people wave branches to ward off approaching evil or terror. The branches are like an extension of our arms, an attempt to protect ourselves from impending horror. What if those waving palm branches were not simply an outburst of hospitality, but also a dark, unconscious attempt to ward off Jesus? [6]

These branches might be both a symbol of devotion and praise as well as a sign of the impending doom that is to come. This interpretation is especially poignant onsidering that, in modern day, the palm branches that are waved around by children as they parade through the sanctuary on

Palm Sunday are later burned. Coincidentally, the ashes created from the burned palm branches are used on Ash Wednesday.

Ash Wednesday is the day that marks the beginning of Lent. It is a time when we remember that we are from the dust, and to the dust we will return.[7]

We take the ashes and mark the sign of the cross on our foreheads or our hands as a symbol which points us to the cross. We see this relationship lived out in one of my favorite hymns, "Sunday's Palms are Wednesday's Ashes" which says:

> *Sunday's palms are Wednesday's ashes*
> *as another Lent begins;*
>
> *Thus we kneel before our Maker*
> *in contrition for our sins.*
>
> *We have marred baptismal pledges*
> *In rebellion gone astray*
>
> *Now returning seek forgiveness*
> *Grant us pardon God this day.*[8]

Maybe a part of Jesus really did see those palm branches as a dark and ominous omen? Maybe he saw them as a warning of how the next few days might go? After all, Jesus has previously predicted his own death three separate times (Mark 8:31; 9:31; 10:32-34). The third time Jesus predicts his death is on his way up to Jerusalem.

They were on the road, going up to Jerusalem, and Jesus was walking ahead of them; they were amazed, and those who followed were afraid. He took the twelve aside again and began to tell them what was to happen to him, saying,

"See, we are going up to Jerusalem, and the Son of Man will be handed over to the chief priests and the scribes, and they will condemn him to death; then they will hand him over to the Gentiles; they will mock him, and spit upon him, and flog him, and kill him; and after three days he will rise again."

(Mark 10:32-34)

Jesus knows the destruction and betrayal that will take place. He is aware of the pain and hurt that will come. Even so, Jesus makes his triumphal entry, and the crowd is there to sing his praises and welcome him into the Holy City. It is really a beautiful moment before things take a drastic turn.

This journey into Jerusalem cannot be stopped. Jesus is on the move. He enters Jerusalem on top of a donkey, in a royal procession, on his way to the cross. His entry confirms his kingship and sets him apart from other earthly kings.

Parades of Power

There are two other royal processions going on in Jerusalem on this very same day. Pontius Pilate and King Herod Antipas are both conducting their own parades as Jesus enters Jerusalem.

Pontius Pilate, the fifth Roman governor of Judea serving under Emperor Tiberius, enters the city of Jerusalem from the west. As he travels from Caesarea by the Sea, it is likely that he has a thousand Roman soldiers accompanying him.

The parade is designed to showcase the force of the mighty and powerful Roman Empire. It is specifically orchestrated to suppress any thought of rebellion from the Jewish people during the Passover festival. This is prudent considering the Passover is a celebration of when the Hebrew people found liberation from slavery in Egypt.

This is a time ripe with thoughts of rebellion and liberation. God has liberated God's people before, perhaps God will do it again? Therefore, Pilate's parade is meant to squash any of kind of thoughts of rebellion from the Jewish people.

Meanwhile, King Herod Antipas, the king of Judea who rules over Galilee and Perea as a client of Rome, enters the city of Jerusalem from the north gate. It is likely that he is traveling with his own group of royal soldiers.

King Herod is also known for using force and violence to suppress the Jewish people. It was King Herod Antipas who had imprisoned John the Baptist and had him beheaded for speaking out against Herod's decision to marry, Herodias, his brother Philip's wife.

Still, Herod is a hopeful figure for many. Despite his use of force, some held on to the hope that the Romans might give power back over to Herod and allow him to rule the entire land. His supporters gather around to celebrate his arrival into Jerusalem.

Note the contrast between Pontius Pilate and Herod Antipas' entry compared to Jesus' entry into Jerusalem. These two rulers are accompanied by a large entourage of soldiers and military figures. Jesus, on the other hand, is accompanied by a small group of disciples. Pilate and Herod enter on horses and chariots. Jesus, by contrast, rides in on a humble donkey. Pilate and Herod enter with the intent to suppress rebellion. Jesus, however, enters as a representation of peace. Pilate and Herod enter as political leaders, reminding all the Jewish people that Rome is in charge. Jesus enters as a man from the peasant city of Nazareth, the son of a carpenter.

Jesus is a very different king than what the Israelites expected. Jesus doesn't come to Jerusalem to rid the people of the Romans. He isn't interested in getting rid of the occupying power.

Jesus is more interested in proclaiming the kingdom of God which lives and dwells in the hearts of believers. He is more interested in delivering people of their sinfulness, shame, guilt, fear, and hopelessness. Jesus is more interested in bringing us from death into life. Jesus doesn't come to defeat the Romans and rule over Israel. Jesus comes to show us the way of the kingdom of God.

I'm sure that when Pilate and Herod hear about Jesus' parade, they aren't very happy. Jesus threatens their authority, and he does a good job of ticking off the Roman Government. Unfortunately, Jesus can't stop there. This triumphal entry leads Jesus directly on a path to the cross.

We are invited to join Jesus as we journey closer to the cross as he enters the Temple and causes all sorts of trouble. We are invited to enter into this story and find our way as we prepare for the Resurrection. We are invited to discover what kind of king Jesus is as we draw closer to his death and resurrection.

Prayer

Loving God, we remember your Son's journey to the cross. We remember how Jesus rode with humility on top of a colt. We remember how Jesus challenged the authorities of the day and called your people to repentance. Jesus is challenging us today as well. Jesus is calling us to repentance. God, give us the strength and courage to sing out shouts of "Hosanna." Allow us to follow Jesus as he journeys closer and closer to the cross; and allow us to receive him as the King of our lives. For we ask all these things in Jesus' name. Amen.

Reflection Questions

1. Jesus asks his disciples to acquire a donkey for him to ride. Have you ever felt like God was asking you to do something strange or out of the ordinary? Has following Jesus ever led you to an unexpected event or encounter?

2. The crowd praises Jesus and welcomes him as a king. How does Jesus' entry into Jerusalem look different than what a normal king might do? What does Jesus' entry on a donkey tell us about the kind of king that Jesus is?

3. Hosanna means "Save us now." What do you think we as individuals, or as a people, need saving from the most?

4. The crowd spreads their cloaks and tree branches on the road ahead of Jesus. What are some ways that we might offer praise to God? How might our praise for Jesus cause us to face challenges?

5. When Jesus entered Jerusalem, many asked who Jesus was. If someone asked you about Jesus, what would be your response? How might you describe your own relationship with Christ?

~

CHAPTER TWO

JESUS THROWS
A TEMPLE TANTRUM

Then they came to Jerusalem. And he entered the temple and began to drive out those who were selling and those who were buying in the temple, and he overturned the tables of the money changers and the seats of those who sold doves; and he would not allow anyone to carry anything through the temple. He was teaching and saying, "Is it not written,

> *'My house shall be called a house*
> *of prayer for all the nations'?*
> *But you have made it a den of robbers."*

And when the chief priests and the scribes heard it, they kept looking for a way to kill him; for they were afraid of him, because the whole crowd was spellbound by his teaching. And when evening came, Jesus and his disciples went out of the city.

(Mark 11:15-19)

The Temple, in Jesus' day, was the focal point of Jerusalem and the center of Jewish life. The Jerusalem Temple was the place to be because it was the mecca of business and commerce, the location for festivals and celebrations, and the place for worship and devotion.

The Jerusalem Temple has a long and rich history. The First Temple in Jerusalem was built in 1,000 B.C.E. by King Solomon, but it was destroyed by King Nebuchadnezzar in 586 B.C.E. during the Babylonian conquest of Jerusalem (2 Kings 25:8-17).

The Second Temple construction started in 538 B.C.E. and was completed in 515 B.C.E. Over half a millennium later, King Herod the Great started a major renovation of the Second Temple in 20 B.C.E., and it was still under construction during the time of Jesus' ministry. Ultimately, the Temple was destroyed again in 70 C.E. by the Romans.[9]

The Second Temple

The Second Temple in Jerusalem (the Temple that existed in Jesus' day) was an impressive structure which had several courts. The innermost court was known as "the Holy of Holies." This was the most sacred space in the Temple. This is where only the high priest entered once a year, on the Day of Atonement, to seek forgiveness for himself and forgiveness on behalf of all the people of Israel.

Outside "the Holy of Holies" was the Court of the Priests. Beyond that was the Court of Israel, and then Court of the Women. Finally, there was the outermost court, the Court of the Gentiles. The Court of the Gentiles was a space where anyone could enter and roam freely, regardless of age, gender, culture, or even religion. It was a place filled with diversity and variety.[10]

In this chapter we will explore how Jesus cleansed the Temple, overturned the tables, and drove out the money changers. After his triumphal entry, Jesus makes his way to the Temple in the Holy City of Jerusalem. As he enters the

Golden Gate into the Temple, it leads him straight into the Court of the Gentiles.

In her book *Entering the Passion of Jesus: A Beginner's Guide to Holy Week*, Amy-Jill Levine describes what the Temple might have looked like when Jesus entered Jerusalem:

> *[The Temple] was a tourist attraction, especially during the pilgrimage festivals. It was very crowded, and it was noisy. The noise was loud and boisterous, and because it was Passover, people were happy because they were celebrating the Feast of Freedom. For many, it was one of the few opportunities to celebrate by eating meat rather than fish. We might think of the setting as a type of vacation for the pilgrims: a chance to leave their homes, to catch up with friends and relatives, to see the "big city," and to feel a special connection with their fellow Jews and with God. It is into this setting that Jesus comes.[11]*

Amid all the celebration and excitement, Jesus is full of dismay, rage, and horror. He sees that the Temple is full of merchants and money changers. The place is packed with oxen, sheep, and doves.

Anyone entering the Temple looking for a quiet place for prayer, reflection, and meditation would be sorely disappointed. The Temple does not seem like a place where one came come to worship God peacefully. No! It is noisy, full of chaos and mayhem. But ironically, all of the ruckus and commotion is completely necessary.

The Function of the Temple

One of the main functions of the Temple is animal sacrifice. According to the Law of Moses, sacrificial animals must be perfect, without blemish. The sacrificial animals can't have any injuries, ailments, or deficiencies. As the Book of Leviticus states:

When anyone offers a sacrifice of well-being to the Lord, in fulfillment of a vow or as a freewill offering, from the herd or from the flock, to be acceptable it must be perfect; there shall be no blemish in it. Anything blind, or injured, or maimed, or having a discharge or an itch or scabs—these you shall not offer to the Lord or put any of them on the altar as offerings by fire to the Lord.

(Leviticus 22:21, 22)

Sacrificial animals were required to be sacrificed without blemish. Only animals who appeared to be flawless were worthy of sacrificing. Therefore, sellers of oxen, sheep, and doves were needed in the Temple. You can't make a sacrifice to God to be forgiven of your sins if you don't have an animal to offer as a sacrifice. Selling these animals in the Temple just makes logistical sense.

Furthermore, the Temple tax had to be paid in Temple coinage. People were coming from all over the place with coins that bore the images of various pagan gods and mortal emperors such as Caesar. The use of these coins goes directly against the commandment forbidding graven images (Exodus 20:4).

Because of this, the money changers were necessary for offerings to be placed in the Temple treasury.[12] This is completely understandable considering the Temple has expenses. They must pay the utility bill. That is simply the cost of doing business.

Jesus, being a Jewish man himself, is familiar with the various Jewish laws and customs. He knows that God requires animal sacrifices. He knows that people have come from miles around to celebrate the Passover. He knows that many people have come to present burnt offerings to God. Jesus has been to the Temple in Jerusalem before! He knows the drill. Nevertheless, these attempts of justification don't seem to do the trick.

Righteous Anger

This encounter in the Temple is one of the few times where we see Jesus get really, really, angry. In a temper tantrum fit for a toddler, Jesus pours out the coins of the money changers, overturns their tables, and speaks out against the dove merchants.

In the Gospel of John's version of this story, Jesus even goes as far as to fashion a whip out cords to drive out the sheep and the cattle (John 2:15). Jesus runs around like Indiana Jones, cracking his whip and chasing out the animals and merchants from the Temple. Jesus almost appears violent as he whips his way through the Temple. Then, in an act of ultimate defiance, Jesus cries out, "My house shall be called a house of prayer for all the nations? But you have made it a den of robbers" (Mark 11:17).

As Eugene Peterson writes in his Bible paraphrase *The Message*, "Stop turning my Father's house into a shopping mall!"

In this rebuke, Jesus is quoting a much longer message from the Prophet Isaiah,

And the foreigners who join themselves to the Lord, to minister to him, to love the name of the Lord, and to be his servants, all who keep the sabbath, and do not profane it, and hold fast my covenant - these I will bring to my holy mountain, and make them joyful in my house of prayer; their burnt offerings and their sacrifices will be accepted on my altar; for my house shall be called a house of prayer for all peoples.

(Isaiah 56:6, 7)

It's important to note that Jesus' criticism of the Temple does not mean that he hates the Temple. It is quite the contrary. Jesus isn't opposed to the purity laws. He doesn't mention anything about the Temple exploiting people or being exclusive. In fact, even Gentiles were welcome to come and worship in the outer court. Jesus' issue is not with the Temple. His real concern is the *attitude* of the people who are coming to the Temple. Jesus is unhappy about people who have come to the Temple while their hearts are far from God.

Additionally, Jesus is upset because he sees that the religious leaders are making money off people by taxing them. They are charging extra to exchange money into the temple coinage. The Temple workers are taking advantage of people who have come to worship God in a space that should be sacred and holy.

The concept of using religion to accumulate wealth is reminiscent of a trend currently sweeping Christianity today, known as the prosperity gospel. This belief wrongfully asserts that faith in God, material wealth, and financial prosperity are linked.

Preachers that proclaim the prosperity gospel offer a message that basically says, "If you follow God (and more importantly if you give generously to a certain ministry fund) then you will be blessed, happy, and fortunate." They say, "If you just become a Christian and send in your money to my ministry, then your life will be easy, and you will be prosperous." They say, "If you give money to God, then God will increase your investment ten-fold"

It appears that the Temple workers in Jesus' day were proponents of this type of ideology. They are charging people extra to make a profit and taking advantage of people who are genuinely striving to get closer to God.

Seeing Jesus this angry, however, makes me a little anxious. Don't get me wrong, I like when Jesus gets angry about the injustice and oppression that exists in our broken world. I appreciate that Jesus speaks up for the poor, the hurting, the marginalized, the outcast, the oppressed, and those who can't speak up for themselves. I like when Jesus speaks up for women who have been mistreated or immigrants who are being denied.

In this story, however, I worry that Jesus' angry words might hit a little too close for comfort. I worry that his anger might have something to do with the way we act as well.

Time to Clean House

Jesus reminds us that the Temple is a house of prayer. It is open to everyone including men, women, slaves, and even Gentiles. The Temple is full of the rich as well as the poor. It truly was a house of prayer for everyone, but there were still parts of the Temple that were closed off to women, Gentiles, and even Jewish males.

Gentiles cannot enter past their court, women cannot enter past theirs, and the Jewish men cannot enter the Holy of Holies, only the high priest can do that. All are welcome in the Temple, but only up to a certain point.

Perhaps Jesus' call for the Temple to be a house of prayer is a commentary on the importance of unrestricted access, not just to the Temple, but to God Almighty! It shouldn't just be the high priest who is able to enter into God's presence. Instead, we should all be able to go straight to God in prayer, enter relationship with God, and ask forgiveness for ourselves.

Still, one can't help but think of how restrictive our own churches can sometimes be. This story forces us to imagine what Jesus might do if he were to enter our church sanctuaries on a Sunday morning.

How might Jesus respond to us and the way that we worship? Would he throw our baskets of offering up into the air? Would he drive us out, just as he did the people who were selling cattle and sheep? Would Jesus think that we are a church that has forgotten its purpose? Would he be happy with our attitudes in worship?

Do our churches illustrate this image of a house of prayer where all people are truly welcome? Have our churches exemplified our call to live as the body of Christ, reaching out to the world? William Hulitt Gloer, Professor of Preaching and Christian Scriptures at Baylor University, states:

The ways of the world invade the church gradually, subtly, never intentionally, always in service of the church and its mission. Soon the church is full of cattle and sheep and turtledoves and money changers.[13]

Maybe it is time for us to clean house? I'm not suggesting that we clear out the furniture in our sanctuaries, or that we dust the pews and vacuum the carpet, and I'm certainly not suggesting that we stop taking up an offering each week! But perhaps this is an invitation for us to reexamine our own hearts and minds. Perhaps it is time for us to clean up our acts.

Community of Believers

In John's Gospel, the disciples come to a deep realization. They hear Jesus' criticism of the Temple turning into a marketplace, and they are then reminded of the words of the Psalmist: "It is zeal for your house that has consumed me" (Psalm 69:9). Some translations say "passion" instead of "zeal."

The disciples make this connection of this Psalm and the Messiah. They realize that the Messiah is consumed with zeal and passion for the house of God. They realize that is why Jesus seems so angry upon entering the Temple. He is living into his role as the Messiah, and he is also offering us a great example of what it looks like to be consumed with passion and zeal.

This is an invitation for us to stop and ask ourselves: What consumes us? What are we passionate about? What are the things that occupy our mind and our time? Are we passionate about our sports teams, our careers, and making money? Has our passion for God's *house* consumed us?

Sometimes we forget why we join for worship services at church each week. We forget what this whole thing is all about. Christians are not just called to go to church or read the Bible (although, these are important things to do). However, as Christians, we are called to do more than that.

Christians are called to *be* the church. If we cannot find ways to reach out to the lost, lonely, and hurting in our community and in our world, then we are completely missing the point. If we are not about reaching people for Jesus and helping to meet people's needs, then we might as well just shut the doors of our churches right now.

The church should be a community of believers who fellowship, worship, and share in God's mission in the world. It's great to have a beautiful building like the Jerusalem Temple, but the church is more than just brick-and-mortar.

A New Way of Doing Things

Jesus makes this big scene in the Temple, challenging the sanctity of the Temple building. He critiques the religious and cultural framework of how things work.

The religious leaders push back. In the Gospel of John, we see a tense exchange occur between Jesus and the religious scholars. They essentially say, "Who do you think you are? What evidence do you have to show that you have the authority to do this?" (John 2:18). They genuinely believe that they are doing things the right way, but in reality they are violating God's purpose. Yet, Jesus coolly responds: "Destroy this temple, and in three days I will raise it up" (John 2:19).

The religious leaders are incensed. They respond by saying, "This temple has been under construction for forty-six years, and will you raise it up in three days?" (John 2:20).

Little did they know that this magnificent and beautiful Temple in Jerusalem would turn into dust and rubble in just a few short years. The Romans will come and destroy it. To this day, the Temple has not been rebuilt. The debris of rocks and pebbles are scattered among the dirt.

When Jesus said he would raise the Temple up in three days, however, he wasn't talking about the building, he was talking about himself. It wasn't until after the resurrection that the disciples looked back and realized what Jesus meant. "*You* destroy the Temple and in three days *I* will raise it up."

It's at this point when the chief priests begin to plot and look for a way to destroy Jesus and take him out of the equation. They succeed, but only for a few short days. Jesus is arrested, convicted, beaten, mocked, and crucified, but Jesus keeps his promise. He stays true to his word. Jesus rises from the dead after three days. The disciples are able to look back and realize that Jesus has come to the earth to make God available in a whole new way.

Jesus is critical of what the Temple in Jerusalem has become. Jesus is tired of the system that is in place. People have gotten so caught up in the chaos and the noise that they fail to recognize the true purpose of the Temple. So, Jesus came to turn it on its head. No longer do people have to get ripped off by a flawed religious system. No longer do people have to present burnt offerings to God in the Temple. No longer do people have to sacrifice animals or get their money changed.

Now, Christ's very own body has become the new location for God. Jesus is where we go to find God because Jesus himself has become the Temple. Not only that, but the Apostle Paul argues that our own bodies have become

Temples because of what Christ had done on the cross. We can enter into a closer relationship with God than ever before through the prompting and power of the Holy Spirit working in our lives. As Paul states:

> *"Or do you not know that your body is a temple of the Holy Spirit within you, which you have from God, and that you are not your own?"*
>
> *(1 Corinthians 6:19)*

Jesus only has a few short days left, but in cleansing the Temple, he shows us a new way of being in relationship with God. In the new Temple, all are truly welcome. In the new Temple, there are no courts restricting certain people from entering. Jesus has a new way of doing things, and no one is excluded.

Prayer

Purifying God, we remember your Son's journey to the Temple. We remember how Jesus challenged the merchants and money changers, driving them out with a whip. Jesus is challenging us today as well. Jesus is calling us to drive out certain things in our own lives that are holding us back. O God, give us the strength and courage to make the necessary changes in our lives. Allow us to follow Jesus as he journeys closer and closer to the cross; and allow us to receive him as the king of our lives. For we ask all these things in Jesus' name. Amen.

Reflection Questions

1. If Jesus were to enter our church sanctuaries on Sunday morning, how do you think he might respond to us and the way that we worship? Would he throw our baskets of offering up into the air? Would Jesus drive us out just as he did the people who were selling cattle and sheep?

2. What do you make of Jesus' anger in the Temple? Does it make you uncomfortable seeing Jesus respond this way? Do you think there are good reasons to be angry?

3. What are you most passionate about? How might you use your passion and zeal to further God's Kingdom and advance the mission of the church?

4. How does the concept of your body acting as a Temple influence your understanding of God and your relationship with God?

5. Despite being on his way to the cross, Jesus spent time healing the blind and the lame in the Temple. How can we go out and be the church in our community and in our world? How can we put other people's needs above our own? How can we serve others as we journey with Jesus to the cross?

CHAPTER THREE

JESUS TEACHES IN THE TEMPLE

Question about Paying Taxes

Then they sent to him some Pharisees and some Herodians to trap him in what he said. And they came and said to him, "Teacher, we know that you are sincere, and show deference to no one; for you do not regard people with partiality, but teach the way of God in accordance with truth. Is it lawful to pay taxes to the emperor, or not? Should we pay them, or should we not?" But knowing their hypocrisy, he said to them, "Why are you putting me to the test? Bring me a denarius and let me see it." And they brought one. Then he said to them, "Whose head is this, and whose title?" They answered, "The emperor's." Jesus said to them, "Give to the emperor the things that are the emperor's, and to God the things that are God's." And they were utterly amazed at him.

Question about the Resurrection

Some Sadducees, who say there is no resurrection, came to him and asked him a question, saying, "Teacher, Moses wrote for us that if a man's brother dies, leaving a wife but no child, the man shall marry the widow and raise up children for his brother. There were seven brothers; the first married and, when he died, left no children; and the second married the widow and died, leaving no children; and the third likewise; none of the seven left children. Last of all the woman herself died. In the resurrection whose wife will she be? For the seven had married her."

Jesus said to them, "Is not this the reason you are wrong, that you know neither the scriptures nor the power of God? For when they rise from the dead, they neither marry nor are given in marriage, but are like angels in heaven. And as for the dead being raised, have you not read in the book of Moses, in the story about the bush, how God said to him, 'I am the God of Abraham, the God of Isaac, and the God of Jacob'? He is God not of the dead, but of the living; you are quite wrong."

Question about the Greatest Commandment

One of the scribes came near and heard them disputing with one another, and seeing that he answered them well, he asked him, "Which commandment is the first of all?" Jesus answered, "The first is, 'Hear, O Israel: the Lord our God, the Lord is one; you shall love the Lord your God with all your heart, and with all your soul, and with all your mind, and with all your strength.' The second is this, 'You shall love your neighbor as yourself.' There is no other commandment greater than these." Then the scribe said to him, "You are right, Teacher; you have truly said that 'he is one, and besides him there is no other'; and 'to love him with all the heart, and with all the understanding, and with all the strength,' and 'to love one's neighbor as oneself,'—this is much more important than all whole burnt offerings and sacrifices." When Jesus saw that he answered wisely, he said to him, "You are not far from the kingdom of God." After that no one dared to ask him any question.

(Mark 12:13-34)

After Jesus cleanses the Temple, he goes back to the village of Bethany and spends the night. (It is likely that Jesus stayed in Bethany each night during the week of the Passover and traveled to Jerusalem during the day). The following day, Jesus returns to the city of Jerusalem and enters the Temple area.

Immediately the chief priests, elders, and scribes begin to question Jesus about his authority. They ask Jesus questions to try to trap him, discredit him, and make him look like a fool.

In this chapter we will explore Jesus' temple teachings as he responds to a series of questions from the religious leaders. We will look at three questions concerning Roman taxation, the resurrection, and the greatest commandment.

A Taxing Question

The Pharisees and the Herodians kickoff with the first question we will explore in this chapter which is about taxation. It is interesting that the Pharisees and the Herodians are working together to try to trap Jesus, considering that these two groups were very different.

The Pharisees were anti-Roman authority and rule. They cared about rule and law of Moses above everything else. The Herodians, however, were supporters of Herod, and they embraced and cooperated with the authority of the Roman government.

These two groups could not be any more different. The only real thing that they have in common is their hatred of Jesus, and it is no surprise they were united in their hatred. This is not surprising considering Jesus is going around and speaking out against these religious leaders. He is challenging their authority, he is calling them out publicly, and he is gaining more and more supporters and followers. He had just cleansed the Temple the previous day, and now the religious leaders have the opportunity to confront Jesus, face to face.

Jesus challenges their order of things. Jesus is so dangerous that the Herodians and the Pharisees plot, plan, and scheme behind closed doors. They have determined that Jesus is so dangerous that they have no other choice than to bring him down, weaken his authority, and secure their authority over his. Therefore, they ask him a series of questions to try to trap him.

When they present their question, the Pharisees and Herodians put on a polite façade like they are trying to catch him with his guard down and throw him off his game. They go to Jesus and say:

> *"Teacher, we know that you are sincere, and show deference to no one; for you do not regard people with partiality, but teach the way of God in accordance with truth. Is it lawful to pay taxes to the emperor, or not? Should we pay them, or should we not?"*
>
> *(Mark 12:14, 15)*

Jesus is publicly asked a very political question about taxes, but notice that Jesus is never one to bring up politics. He doesn't seem too concerned with what the Roman government and officials are doing. He never brings up political issues in the Bible. Instead, he is much more concerned about the kingdom of God, not the reign of Caesar.

This topic of discussion comes up, not because Jesus wants to talk about it, but because it is a controversial topic. The religious leaders are clearly trying to trap him.

During the election cycle candidates are asked very difficult questions, and sometimes their answers can cause them to lose their chances at winning the election. We see this happen on the debate stage, in interviews, and on the campaign trail. Sometimes these questions are specifically designed to throw the candidates off their game, to trick them, and cause their downfall.

Jesus is almost like a candidate in an election year who is asked a very straightforward, "yes or no," question. "Should we pay taxes to Caesar or not?" This question puts Jesus in a very real dilemma.

On the one hand, if Jesus speaks out against paying taxes, then he might be reported to the Roman government officials and could be arrested.

On the other hand, if Jesus affirms the practice of paying taxes, he would essentially be endorsing a corrupt government that takes advantage of his fellow Jewish people.

Paying taxes during the days of Jesus was very different than it is today. It was even more controversial back then, because the people of the Jewish faith believed that even possessing a Roman coin was blasphemous and a practice in idolatry (Deuteronomy 4:15, 16). If Jesus were to affirm paying taxes, then many of his followers might consider Jesus to be a traitor and pull their support from him.

When Jesus is asked about taxes, however, he sees right through the question and realizes that it is a trap. Jesus calls out his questioners, saying, "Why are you putting me to the test? Bring me a denarius and let me see it... Whose head is this and whose title?" (Mark 12:15, 16). Jesus essentially says, "Show me the money."

This is a brilliant move by Jesus. By asking "Whose name is on the coin?" Jesus has completely changed the conversation from being about taxes to being about possession and identity.

They religious leaders confess that it is Caesar's name on the coin. And with that, Jesus tells them, "Give to Caesar the things that are Caesar's, and to God the things that are God's" (Mark 12:17).

With this answer, Jesus avoids the open trap set before him. But notice that Jesus doesn't fully answer the question. Jesus has a habit of rarely answering questions with a direct response. Instead, Jesus is much more interested in asking questions, not answering them.

Throughout the Gospels, Jesus asks a total of 307 questions. By contrast, other people ask Jesus a total of 183 questions, and of those 183 questions that he is asked, Jesus only explicitly answers 3 of them.[14]

Needless to say, this is not one of the 3 occasions where Jesus directly answers the question. Sure, Jesus says, "Give to Caesar the things that are Caesar's and to God the things that are God's." (Mark 12:17). However, Jesus never specifies what belongs to Caesar and what belongs to God.

Ironically, Jesus' so called "answer" only leads to more questions. What does Jesus mean by this? Should we pay taxes, or not? What belongs to Caesar? What belongs to God?

For any serious scholar of the Hebrew Scriptures, the answer is obvious. After all, the Psalmist clearly defines what belongs to God, and it is absolutely everything – the earth, the world, and all that is in it. As the Psalmist writes:

> *The earth is the Lord's and all that is in it, the world, and those who live in it; for he has founded it on the seas, and established it on the rivers.*

> *(Psalm 24:1, 2)*

This Psalm causes us to consider several probing questions. How do we balance our faith and our politics? How do we navigate this political world that we live in without worshiping it as a false idol? What (or who) do we look to for hope, help, and healing? What do we look to for morality and guidance? Who is really our Savior? Is it Caesar, or is it God? These are the essential question that Jesus is addressing, and they are questions that we must ask of ourselves.

Jesus tells us that we should pay our taxes, but we should also realize that our money and American values are material and earthly. We give a percentage of our money, and we might even think to ourselves, "This is my money. I earned it. It's mine. I can do what I want with it." But then, we must ask the question, "What belongs to God?"

John Wesley, the founder of the Methodist Movement, had a lot of good things to say when it came to the use of money. In his sermon "On the Use of Money," Wesley proposed three financial rules or guidelines to follow, "Earn all you can, save all you can, and give all you can."[15] Wesley did not let the material world influence his faith, but he let his faith dictate the way he lived in the material world.

Christ does not want a part of our lives. Christ wants it all. Everything we are and everything we have truly belongs to God. When we breathe our last breath, we do not carry with us a coin with the image of Caesar ingrained on it. Instead, our very souls are made in the image of God. We bear the image of the God who created us, formed us, and breathed the breath of life into us.

Jesus points out that Caesar's coin has Caesar's image on it. Caesar's name is inscribed on it. Therefore, it belongs to Caesar. In doing that, Jesus is also pointing out that our lives are different.

We belong to God because we are created in God's divine image. God's name is inscribed on us in our baptisms. Everything we are belongs to God because we bear God's image. The Pharisees and Herodians hear Jesus' answer to this first question, and they are utterly amazed.

The Resurrection

In another attempt to trap Jesus, the Sadducees go to him with a question about the resurrection. The Sadducees ask him a question about the afterlife even though they do not believe in the resurrection. As the cheesy preacher joke goes, this is why they are so "Sad-you-see." They are trying to discredit Jesus in front of the crowd by proposing a completely unlikely scenario that seems impossible to answer. They ask:

"Teacher, Moses wrote for us that if a man's brother dies, leaving a wife but no child, the man shall marry the widow and raise up children for his brother. There were seven brothers; the first married and, when he died, left no children; and the second married the widow and died, leaving no children; and the third likewise; none of the

seven left children. Last of all the woman herself died. In the resurrection whose wife will she be? For the seven had married her."

(Mark 12:19-23)

In their question, the Sadducees refer to the Jewish practice of levirate marriage. This law, which is spelled out in Deuteronomy 25:5-10, states that if a woman's husband dies before she conceives a child, then the husband's brother is supposed to marry the woman and birth a child on the deceased husband's behalf. In this hypothetical situation presented by the Sadducees, a woman's husband dies, and she marries seven brothers in succession. The Sadducees want to know who the woman will be married to in the afterlife.

In response to this, Jesus alludes to a passage in Isaiah and essentially calls them out for knowing nothing about the Scriptures or the power of God. As the prophet Isaiah says, "From ages past no one has heard, no ear has perceived, no eye has seen any God besides you, who works for those who wait for him" (Isaiah 64:4).

Jesus claims that there will be no marriage in the afterlife, saying, "For when people rise from the dead, they neither marry nor are given in marriage but are like angels in heaven" (Mark 12:25). Things will look different in the resurrection.

Finally, Jesus ends his brief response by recalling Moses and the story of the burning bush. He reminds them that God is a God of the living, not the dead. In other words, the kingdom of God is primarily about what we are experiencing right here and right now.

The Resurrection of Lazarus

It is entirely likely that the Sadducees asked Jesus this question in response to hearing about the resurrection of Lazarus. In this story, which is only told in the Gospel of John, Jesus' friend Lazarus has died. His sisters Mary and Martha are upset with Jesus, and for good reason. Jesus had been warned that Lazarus, was sick.

Even though Jesus loves Lazarus, he still stays where he is for two more days. Jesus doesn't seem too concerned about his dear friend's fate. He knows that Lazarus will be okay, and he even tells his disciples, "This illness does not lead to death; rather, it is for God's glory, so that the Son of God may be glorified through it" (John 11:4).

When Jesus finally gets to the village of Bethany, Lazarus has been dead for four days; and, of course, Mary and Martha are upset. Martha is clearly frustrated when she says, "Lord, if you had been here, my brother would not have died" (John 11:21).

Unfortunately, death is a reality. From the very beginning, in the book of Genesis, God says, "You are dust, and to dust you shall return" (Genesis 3:19). Life is temporary and fragile, but when it happens to someone close to us it can shake us to the core and rattle our faith. We state the infamous question, "What sort of God would allow this to happen?"

Even though Martha is experiencing pain and frustration at the death of her brother, you can hear the hope when she says, "But even now I know that God will give you whatever you ask of him" (John 11:22). Despite her grief, Martha still believes in the power of resurrection and her belief is affirmed when Jesus says:

"Your brother will rise again... I am the resurrection and the life. Those who believe in me, even though they die, will live, and everyone who lives and believes in me will never die."

(John 11:25, 26)

Then Mary is called to come to Jesus, and Mary repeats word for word exactly what her sister had said, "Lord, if you had been here, my brother would not have died" (John 11:32); however, something different happens this time.

When Jesus sees Mary weeping, he begins to weep as well. He spends this moment grieving and morning with Mary, expressing his humanity. He shares this moment of sorrow with Mary. As the Presbyterian minister and theologian, Cynthia Jarvis states:

Jesus weeps, his tears constituting the only theological response we often can make when called to the side of the grieving. To another's lament and longing for a reason from on high, we speak of the God who weeps with us. Jesus wept over Jerusalem, at Lazarus' tomb, and in the Garden of Gethsemane. Jesus shares in our pain.[16]

When Jesus comes to Lazarus' tomb he is moved with compassion and commands that the stone from his tomb be taken away. At this point, Martha begins to panic. Martha, who had just talked to Jesus about the resurrection, says, "Lord, already there is a stench because he has been dead four days." (John 11:39). Martha can only think of one reason who Jesus wants to open Lazarus' tomb – Jesus must want to look on the face of his dead friend one last time. She doesn't realize that Jesus is about to perform a miracle.

Jesus responds saying, "Did I not tell you that if you believed, you would see the glory of God?" (John 11:40). Then Jesus offers a public prayer as they take the stone away, calling out to God so that others will believe that he is indeed the Messiah.

As Jesus shouts, "Lazarus, come out," the most amazing thing happens. Lazarus comes out of the tomb in a spooky scene fit for a Stephen King novel. Imagine a thick layer of fog as Lazarus staggers forth, looking like a zombie or mummy, because he has cloth wrapped around his face, hands, and feet. With that, the narrative ends abruptly with Jesus saying, "Unbind him, and let him go" (John 11:44).

The resurrection of Lazarus reminds us that there is hope in the end for those who are suffering. There is hope for the impoverished, persecuted, threatened, rejected, abused, marginalized, oppressed, and isolated. Death is not the final word.

Little did the Sadducees know, in just a few short days, Jesus would perform this miracle once again. Little did they know, Jesus would be the resurrection himself, and he would resurrect our hearts.

The resurrection of Lazarus foretells Jesus' own Resurrection. As Jesus himself says, "I am the resurrection and the life. Those who believe in me, even though they die, will live, and everyone who lives and believes in me will never die" (John 11:25, 26).

Greatest Commandment

While teaching in the Temple Jesus is asked another question concerning the greatest of the Jewish laws and commandments. One of the teachers of religious law realizes that Jesus is brilliantly answering all the questions that are being thrown at him. So, he asks him, "Which commandment is the first of all?" (Mark 12:28).

Our first inclination in hearing this question might be to consider the Ten Commandments which are the primary rules that were given to the Jewish people by Moses on Mt. Sinai. The Ten Commandments state:

1. I am the Lord your God, who brought you out of the land of Egypt, out of the house of slavery; you shall have no other gods before me.

2. You shall not make for yourself an idol, whether in the form of anything that is in heaven above or that is on the earth beneath or that is in the water under the earth.

3. You shall not make wrongful use of the name of the Lord your God, for the Lord will not acquit anyone who misuses his name.

4. Remember the Sabbath day and keep it holy.

5. Honor your father and your mother, so that your days may be long in the land that the Lord your God is giving you.

6. You shall not murder.

7. You shall not commit adultery.

8. You shall not steal.

9. You shall not bear false witness against your neighbor.

10. You shall not covet your neighbor's house; you shall not covet your neighbor's wife, male or female slave, ox, donkey, or anything that belongs to your neighbor.

The Commandments are foundational to living out the Jewish faith. Surely one of these rules would earn the spot at the top. The Ten Commandments, however, are not the only rules and laws presented to the Jewish people. In fact, there are 613 commandments in the Hebrew Scriptures that are recognized in the Jewish traditions. Therefore, Jesus has a lot more commandments to choose from!

This is one of the few times where Jesus answers a question directly. In response to this question, Jesus cites an Old Testament law known as "the Shema" which says:

"Hear, O Israel: The Lord is our God, the Lord alone. You shall love the Lord your God with all your heart and with all your soul and with all your might. Keep these words that I am commanding you today in your heart. Recite them to your children and talk about them when you are at home and when you are away, when you lie down and when you rise. Bind them as a sign on your hand, fix them as an emblem on your forehead, and write them on the doorposts of your house and on your gates."

(Deuteronomy 6:4-9)

This is a prayer that is recited by the Jewish people as often as three times a day, and it is foundational to the Jewish faith. Jesus takes the basis of the Shema and builds on it. Jesus proclaims the greatest commandment saying:

"The first is, 'Hear, O Israel: the Lord our God, the Lord is one; you shall love the Lord your God with all your heart, and with all your soul, and with all your mind, and with all your strength. The second is this, 'You shall love your neighbor as yourself.' There is no other commandment greater than these."

(Mark 12: 29-31)

Jesus claims that love is the center of the greatest commandment of all, and the religious teacher, surprisingly, is in full agreement.

The Good Samaritan

In the Gospel of Luke, Jesus shares a similar conversation with a legal expert leading Jesus to the tell the parable of the Good Samaritan (Luke 10:25-37). The story is about a man who is traveling on a dangerous road from Jerusalem to Jericho. It is a treacherous road full of twists, turns, and blind spots. It is a perfect place for robbers and thieves to target a lonely traveler, and that is exactly what happens.

As the man is walking along the desert road he is attacked by robbers. He is stripped, beaten, and left half-dead on the side of the road. After some time, the man looks up and sees a priest walking toward him. The priest is a member of the religious system in Israel. He is a holy man who works in the Temple and performs sacrifices on the altar.

Surely the priest will stop and help him; however, the man lies there and watches as the priest passes by on the other side of the road. But let's not be unfair to the priest. After all, this is a dangerous road, and priests are busy. They have a lot on their plates. This priest probably just had somewhere more important he had to be.

The man on the road is still deserted. He is lying there with no hope. After some more time goes by, the man looks up and sees a Levite walking toward him. The Levite is a member of the tribe of Levi. He's given a very special religious status. He sings the Psalms during Temple and serves as a teacher and a judge. Again, this is another holy man.

Although the priest didn't stop, surely the Levite will stop and help; however, the man lies there and watches as the Levite passes by on the other side of the road. Again, let's not be unfair to the Levite. After all, Levites are busy. They too have a lot on their plates. He probably just has somewhere he has to be.

At this point, the man is dehydrated, the sun is burning his skin, and he has lost a lot of blood. Some more time goes by, and he uses what little strength he has left to lift his head long enough to see a no-good, despised, Samaritan walking toward him. He is the last person the man wants to see in such a vulnerable position.

He sees this Samaritan and probably thinks, "Well, there's no hope. I'm going to die here. There is no way that a Samaritan would stop and help a Jew like myself." Surprisingly, the Samaritan sees the dying man on the side of the road (and unlike the Priest and the Levite) the Samaritan is the one who has compassion for the man.

The Good Samaritan binds up the man's wounds, puts him on his own donkey, and takes him to the nearest inn. When they arrive, the Samaritan pays for the man's room, and he even covers all the man's medical bills. This Good Samaritan helps a complete stranger, putting the needs of another person above his own.

This parable points out something that is important for all of us. So often, the sin that we are most guilty of is the sin of omission. Sometimes our most grievous sins are when we fail to do the right thing. The Priest and the Levite didn't really do anything wrong, but their mistake was failing to do something right. They saw a need, and instead of helping, they ignored it. In response to this parable, Martin Luther King, Jr. once said:

The first question which the priest and the Levite asked was: "If I stop to help this man, what will happen to me?" But by the very nature of his concern, the good Samaritan reversed the question: "If I do not stop to help this man, what will happen to him?"[17]

It is hard to put someone else's needs above our own. It is hard to risk yourself for the sake of another. Our world is in desperate need of this kind of neighborly love. We are called to express our love for others when they find themselves in difficult situations. Besides, don't you want someone to help you when you find yourself in a difficult situation?

Jesus invites us to follow the example of the Good Samaritan. Jesus is calling us to action, telling us to offer compassion, show mercy, extend kindness, to love God, and to love our neighbor.

While in the Temple, Jesus has several exchanges with the religious leaders. He talks about paying taxes, he talks about the resurrection, and he talks about the greatest commandment. Years later, we are still amazed at the authority and wisdom of Jesus' teachings.

Prayer

Generous God, we remember how Jesus was challenged and questioned by the religious leaders of his day, but we see how Jesus answers each of these questions with authority. God, you are the creator of the universe, and everything we see on this earth is made possible because of you. Help us to recognize your power and authority and help us to follow your Greatest Commandment of love. O God, give us the strength and courage to make the necessary changes in our lives. Allow us to follow Jesus as he journeys closer and closer to the cross; and allow us to receive him as the king of our lives. For we ask all these things in Jesus' name. Amen.

Reflection Questions

1. Does Jesus' call to give to Caesar what is Caesar's and give to God what is God's challenge the way you prioritize things? Does it challenge the way you understand your allegiance to America and your allegiance to Christ?

2. John Wesley encouraged others to earn all they can, save all they can, and give all they can. What are ways that you might spend, save, and give to your church and community?

3. How might you allow your faith to influence the way you spend your money, instead of allowing your money to dictate your faithfulness?

4. Jesus says that the greatest commandment is to love God and neighbor. What are some ways that you can live out this commandment in your own life?

5. What does Jesus' portrayal of the Good Samaritan tell you about God's generosity? How might God's generosity help motivate you to be generous to your neighbors?

CHAPTER FOUR

JESUS IS
ANNOINTED

While he was at Bethany in the house of Simon the leper, as he sat at the table, a woman came with an alabaster jar of very costly ointment of nard, and she broke open the jar and poured the ointment on his head. But some were there who said to one another in anger, "Why was the ointment wasted in this way? For this ointment could have been sold for more than three hundred denarii, and the money given to the poor." And they scolded her. But Jesus said, "Let her alone; why do you trouble her? She has performed a good service for me. For you always have the poor with you, and you can show kindness to them whenever you wish; but you will not always have me. She has done what she could; she has anointed my body beforehand for its burial. Truly I tell you, wherever the good news is proclaimed in the whole world, what she has done will be told in remembrance of her."

Then Judas Iscariot, who was one of the twelve, went to the chief priests in order to betray him to them. When they heard it, they were greatly pleased, and promised to give him money. So he began to look for an opportunity to betray him.

(Mark 14:3-9)

On June 5, 2022, during my ordination service, I stood before the Holston Annual Conference in Stuart Auditorium at Lake Junaluska, North Carolina. Surrounded by fellow clergy and laity, I knelt before Bishop Wallace-Padgett as she placed her hands on my head and said:

Almighty God, pour upon Andrew Curtis Lay the Holy Spirit, for the office and work of an elder in Christ's holy church. Amen.

Then, as I rested my hands on the Holy Bible, she placed her hands over mine and proclaimed:

Andrew Curtis Lay, take authority as an elder to preach the Word of God, to administer the Holy Sacraments and to order the life of the Church; in the name of the Father, and of the Son, and of the Holy Spirit.

At that moment I felt a strong sense of anointing in my life. I felt that God truly was pouring out God's Spirit upon me. It was a powerful and holy moment that will be with me for the rest of my life.

In this chapter we will explore the anointing that Jesus receives as he accepts his role as Messiah, embraces his journey to the cross, and prepares for his burial in the tomb.

The Unnamed Woman

At this point in the story, Jesus returns to the village of Bethany following his teaching session in the Temple. In Bethany he shares in a meal at the home of Simon, a man who previously had leprosy. While in Simon's home, Jesus receives a special blessing as he prepares for his own death and resurrection.

Bethany is not only the location of Simon's home, but it is also the town of Jesus' dear friends Martha, Mary, and Lazarus (Lazarus' resurrection is mentioned in the previous chapter). John's account of Jesus' anointing includes these friends at this dinner (John 11:2).

According to John's Gospel, Lazarus is seated alongside Jesus at the dinner table, while Martha is diligently cooking, cleaning, and serving the meal. Her sister, Mary, however, is doing something completely out of the ordinary. She goes to Jesus and extravagantly anoints his feet with expensive oil.

The Synoptic Gospels (Matthew, Mark, and Luke) describe the encounter of Jesus' anointing in different ways. For example, Matthew and Mark's Gospels share about an unnamed woman who prepares Jesus for his burial by anointing Jesus' head (Matthew 26:1-13; Mark 14:3-9).

Luke's Gospel, on the other hand, talks of an unnamed woman who anoints Jesus' feet with her tears and dries them with her hair. There appears to be no connection to Jesus' burial or the passion narrative in Luke's account (Luke 7:36-49).

Whether these accounts are all a retelling of the same event or different events, we cannot ignore the similarities.

While Jesus is reclined at the table, a woman brings forth an alabaster jar of expensive perfume made from essence of nard. Nard is an oil that comes from the root of the nard plant which grows in the mountains of northern India. It is exotic and extravagant, something that is not easy to obtain.

She takes the fragrant oil and anoints Jesus by pouring it on him. This moment is incredibly intimate and personal. In the woman's act of anointing Jesus, she is expressing complete devotion and faithfulness to her Messiah. This intimate act of anointing Jesus with oil is reminiscent of when Jesus washes his disciples' feet.

Foot Washing

In the Gospel of John, while Jesus is sharing in the Passover festival with his disciples, he offers a precursor to his act of sacrifice on the cross by washing the feet of his disciples. This is the ultimate act of humility. Jesus washes the disciples' feet much like when Mary anointed Jesus' feet with perfume which she wiped with her hair.

Imagine Jesus standing up from the table, rolling up his sleeves, tying an apron around his waist, and grabbing a basin and pitcher of water. Imagine the shock of the disciples when Jesus says, "Okay, take off your sandals so I can wash your filthy, dust-covered feet."

Peter is upset by Jesus' offer and tries to refuse him the privilege of washing his feet. It just doesn't seem right to Peter that Jesus would wash his feet; it should be the other way around. Peter says, "You will never wash my feet" (John 13:8a).

However, Jesus is insistent because he wants to teach his disciples something important. He tells Peter, "Unless I wash you, you have no share with me" (John 13:8b). At this Peter realizes the significance of this moment, and he asks to be cleansed from head to toe, but Jesus responds, "One who has bathed does not need to wash, except for the feet, but is entirely clean" (John 13:10).

Jesus goes around to each of his followers and washes their feet, one by one. Then, after he washes their feet, he says:

Do you know what I have done to you? You call me Teacher and Lord, and you are right, for that is what I am. So if I, your Lord and Teacher, have washed your feet, you also ought to wash one another's feet. For I have set you an example, that you also should do as I have done to you. Very truly, I tell you, slaves are not greater than their master, nor are messengers greater than the one who sent them. If you know these things, you are blessed if you do them.

(John 13:12-17)

Jesus chooses to serve his disciples in a personal and intimate way, but we sometimes have a hard time doing this ourselves. We sometimes have a hard time accepting help and allowing others to serve us. We often want to portray this image to the world that says, "I have it all figured out. I can do it all myself. I don't need any help." Jesus, however, teaches us the importance of accepting acts of service from others with gratitude.

Jesus also teaches us that it is important to offer acts of service to others as well. We are to serve in ways that are up close and personal. It's not just about writing a check or dropping off some food to someone, but it is also about building relationships. As followers of Christ, we are called to get to know people, hear their stories, and enter into their lives in vulnerable and intimate ways. We are invited to find ways to serve others in a real and meaningful way.

The Anointed King

When the unnamed woman anoints Jesus, she is acknowledging Jesus' role as the Messiah. The Hebrew word for "Messiah" is the word *mashiach* which literally means "anointed" or "anointed one."[18] Jesus is identified and set apart by God and for God's purposes. In this story, Jesus lives into his role as the anointed king, the Messiah, the Savior, and the Son of God.

The anointing of a king is a concept that is present all throughout Scripture. We can recall the Old Testament story when God instructed the prophet Samuel to anoint Saul as Israel's first king.

Samuel took a vial of oil and poured it on his head, and kissed him (Saul); he said, "The Lord has anointed you ruler over his people Israel. You shall reign over the people of the Lord and you will save them from the hand of their enemies all around.

(1 Samuel 10:1)

The anointing of Israel's first king started a long tradition of kings that were anointed by the prophets and priests. King after king is anointed and set apart by God to rule and reign over the people of Israel. In fact, this tradition of anointing kings and queens is still popular today in many cultures and traditions.

One of my favorite television shows is the hit Netflix series *The Crown*. This show is a semi-historical drama about the reign of Queen Elizabeth II. I am completely fascinated with this inside look into the history of the Royal Family.

In the fifth episode of the first season, Princess Elizabeth is anointed with oil during her coronation as she officially becomes the Queen of England.

Although the coronation itself was televised, the anointing of the monarch was too sacred to be shown on television. Therefore, the actual footage from 1953 completely omits the anointing during the broadcast.

In the show, however, we get a small glimpse into what that anointing might have looked like. The Archbishop of Canterbury pours the chrism from the ampulla onto a spoon and anoints Elizabeth's hands, chest, and forehead while saying:

As kings, priests, and prophets were anointed, and as Solomon was anointed king by Zadok the priest and Nathan the prophet so be thou, anointed, blessed, and consecrated Queen over the peoples whom the Lord thy God has given thee to rule and govern.[19]

When I was watching this episode, I couldn't help but feel a sense of awe and reverence. It was compelling to see this young woman be anointed in such a holy and sacred ceremony.

One can't help but notice the difference between the anointing of Queen Elizabeth II and Jesus' anointing. Jesus is not anointed by a prophet, or a priest, or the Archbishop of Canterbury. Instead, an ordinary woman anoints Jesus. In a simple and humble coronation service, Jesus is anointed in an unexpected way, in an unexpected place, and by an unexpected person.

I doubt that the unnamed woman understood the gravity of who Jesus actually is and what Jesus is about do, but she knows that there is something special about Jesus.

The beauty of this moment is that the woman is expressing an outpouring of love-filled hospitality and devotion. She has the gumption to be the one to perform this holy and sacred ceremony for Jesus.

Perfume and the Poor

Not everyone in the house approves of the woman's actions. In fact, some of the people at the table are indignant. John's Gospel specifically names Judas Iscariot (one of Jesus' disciples, the keeper of the common purse, and the one who will betray Jesus) as one who speaks out. Judas openly voices his disapproval, saying the anointing of oil is a waste of a precious resource (John 12:4-6).

The objectors have a point. The woman has used up an entire jar of perfume that cost the equivalent of an entire year's wage. Is it really necessary to use a whole pound of expensive perfume? The perfume could have been sold and the money could have been given to the poor. Isn't this what Jesus would have wanted?

Everything Jesus has done leading up to this point suggests that Jesus cares about the poor and powerless, the lost and lonely.

Throughout his ministry, Jesus eats with sinners, prostitutes, and tax collectors. Jesus feeds multitudes of people with only five loaves and two fish. Jesus heals the lame, the blind, and the diseased without ever asking for a cent in return. He exercises demons, saves a woman from being stoned for adultery, and preaches to the Gentiles.

Jesus is constantly reaching out to the lost, lonely, and hurting in the world. Therefore, giving money to the poor instead of using it on expensive perfume is in keeping with Jesus' actions and teachings.

John's Gospel, however, gives us the inside scoop into Judas Iscariot's true intentions. Judas complains about the use of this perfume, not because he is concerned for the poor and the needy, but because he wants to keep the money for himself. Jesus sees through these complaints, and he responds by getting straight to the heart of the matter. Jesus says:

"Let her alone; why do you trouble her? She has performed a good service for me. For you always have the poor with you, and you can show kindness to them whenever you wish; but you will not always have me. She has done what she could; she has anointed my body beforehand for its burial. Truly I tell you, wherever the good news is proclaimed in the whole world, what she has done will be told in remembrance of her."

(Mark 14:6-9)

Jesus has nothing against the poor. He is not suggesting that we should stop helping the poor and needy among us. Jesus is not neglecting the poor, but he is simply giving attention to the moment at hand. He is preparing for his own death.

Anointing for Burial

The anointing of Jesus ultimately anticipates Jesus' future burial, pointing to his death. In the Jewish tradition, kings are not the only ones who are anointed. The dead are also anointed before they are buried. When Jesus says that he has been anointed for the day of his burial, he uses the Greek word *myrizo* which means "to anoint with myrrh a body for burial."[20] Myrrh was used in incense as well as in anointing oil, and it was often used to embalm dead bodies.

Myrrh is one of the three gifts that Jesus received following his birth. According to Matthew's Gospel, the Wise Men, or the magi, travel to Bethlehem from the east to pay homage to the newborn king. They bring gifts of gold, frankincense, and myrrh (Matthew 2:1-12).

Each of these gifts foretell a certain aspect of Jesus' life and ministry. The gift of gold foretells Jesus' role as a king. The gift of frankincense foretells Jesus' role as a priest. The gift of myrrh foretells of Jesus' death and resurrection. From the very beginning, Jesus was brought to this world to come as a living sacrifice. He comes into this world to live and die for us as the ultimate sacrifice.

The unnamed woman listens to Jesus, takes a leap of faith, and anoints Jesus in an act of extravagant love and devotion.

During the season of Lent, we are invited to participate in extravagant acts of love and devotion. How might we find ways to serve others? How can we follow the example of Jesus who was willing to wash his disciples' feet? How can we embody the unnamed woman's act of service by giving of ourselves in extravagant ways? It is often when we engage in acts of mercy and service for others that we receive an anointing ourselves.

This event in the Gospel story pushes the narrative forward and prepares us for what will soon take place. From there, Judas Iscariot goes to the leading priests to arrange the betrayal of Jesus. For Judas, the anointing is the final straw that breaks the camel's back. Now, we continue the journey from palms, to passion, to resurrection.

Prayer

Almighty God, we remember when your Son was anointed by Mary. We remember how Jesus was recognized for his role as Messiah, and we also remember how Jesus embraced his role as one who came to die. Help us to be extravagant in our worship of you. O God, give us the strength and courage to make the necessary changes in our lives. Allow us to follow Jesus as he journeys closer and closer to the cross; and allow us to receive him as the king of our lives. For we ask all these things in Jesus' name. Amen.

Reflection Questions

1. Jesus is the "Messiah" (the anointed one). Mary recognizes his role as king. How does this understanding of Jesus as the anointed king deepen your understanding of Jesus?

2. Jesus is king, but he also embraces his role as the one who was born to die. Mary anoints Jesus with myrrh (myrrh was often used to anoint dead corpses for burial). How does this understanding of Jesus' burial preparation deepen your understanding of Jesus?

3. Judas criticizes Mary for wasting expensive perfume by anointing Jesus' feet. Have you ever been criticized for something good that you have done?

4. Jesus says that the poor will always be with us. If this is the case, what is the church's responsibility when it comes to the issue of poverty? How might Jesus be challenging us to reach out to the poor and powerless?

5. In this story the unnamed woman acts extravagantly in her devotion to Jesus as the Messiah. How might we engage in extravagant acts of love and devotion for God and others?

CHAPTER FIVE

JESUS AT
THE LAST SUPPER

On the first day of Unleavened Bread, when the Passover lamb is sacrificed, his disciples said to him, "Where do you want us to go and make the preparations for you to eat the Passover?" So he sent two of his disciples, saying to them, "Go into the city, and a man carrying a jar of water will meet you; follow him, and wherever he enters, say to the owner of the house, 'The Teacher asks, where is my guest room where I may eat the Passover with my disciples?' He will show you a large room upstairs, furnished and ready. Make preparations for us there." So the disciples set out and went to the city, and found everything as he had told them; and they prepared the Passover meal.

When it was evening, he came with the twelve. And when they had taken their places and were eating, Jesus said, "Truly I tell you, one of you will betray me, one who is eating with me." They began to be distressed and to say to him one after another, "Surely, not I?" He said to them, "It is one of the twelve, one who is dipping bread into the bowl with me. For the Son of Man goes as it is written of him, but woe to that one by whom the Son of Man is betrayed! It would have been better for that one not to have been born."

While they were eating, he took a loaf of bread, and after blessing it he broke it, gave it to them, and said, "Take; this is my body." Then he took a cup, and after giving thanks he gave it to them, and all of them drank from it. He said to them, "This is my blood of the covenant, which is poured out for many. Truly I tell you, I will never again drink of the fruit of the vine until that day when I drink it new in the kingdom of God."

(Mark 14:12-25)

There is a sense of community that is felt when folks are sitting around a table, eating food, and sharing with some good company. Somehow, being around food brings people together. Food is such an important part of what it means to be in community with others. In fact, the word "companion" comes from the Latin term *companio* which was used to describe "someone with whom you share a meal."[21]

At the center of every holiday celebration there is a meal. Thanksgiving, for example, is a time for families to come together to eat turkey, dressing, and all the fixings. Food can trigger powerful memories, deep feelings, and strong emotions. When you smell some of your favorite dishes, it can make you feel nostalgic and sentimental. Food can remind you about fond memories of loved ones, and food can be an effective way to connect you to our past.

Sharing in a meal at the table is not complete without conversation. When you are at the dinner table with your family, you talk about what went on at work or at school that day. You share funny stories and discuss important issues and topics: like sports, pop culture, and the meaning of life. You can solve all the world's problems when you are sitting and talking at the dinner table. Sitting around the table is where deep discussions take place, because communal dining is central to the human experience.

Jesus' Appetite

Meals also play an important role throughout Jesus' earthly ministry. Jesus attends a banquet at Levi's house (Luke 5:27-29), he eats dinner at Simon the Pharisee's house (Luke 7:36-50), Jesus feeds the multitude (Matthew 14:13-211; Mark 6:30-44; Luke 9:10-17; John 6:1-15), and Jesus shares in a meal at Mary and Martha's house (Luke 10:38-42; John 12:2).

Jesus is constantly eating with people. He eats with tax collectors, Pharisees, sinners, friends, and his disciples. Jesus is constantly breaking bread with people from all walks of life. Jesus understands the importance and the power of food. As preacher and theologian, Andrew Foster Connors, says:

> *If Jesus had not traveled by foot so far and so often, it is quite possible that Jesus would have been a little chunkier than he appears in most stained-glass windows.*[22]

Jesus likes to eat. In fact, he develops a reputation for eating, drinking, and feasting, and he is criticized for his eating habits. As the Gospel of Luke states, "The Son of Man has come eating and drinking, and you say, 'Look, a glutton and a drunkard, a friend of tax collectors and sinners!'" (Luke 7:34).

I've never been accused of being a drunkard or a glutton. I think with the portion sizes we have in the United States, you would have to work hard to earn the title of glutton. It's obvious that Jesus really enjoys eating with people, not just because he loves food, but because he understands the power of sharing a meal with others. Jesus realizes how community can be formed around the table, and Jesus eats with people from all walks of life.

The Passover Seder

In this chapter, we will explore the meal that Jesus shares with his disciples during the Last Supper (Matthew 26:17-29; Mark 14:12-25; Luke 22:7-38; and 1 Corinthians 11:23-25). The Last Supper is perhaps the most important meal in all the Gospels. In the Upper Room, Jesus gathers around the table with his closest friends, these twelve disciples that have been by his side for the past three years, as they share in the Passover Celebration.

So far, there is nothing strange about this event. The Passover Celebration is a Jewish festival that is embraced by all the people of faith in Jerusalem. As we discussed in chapter one, thousands of people gather in the Holy City of Jerusalem every year to celebrate the Passover festival and remember when God led the Israelites out of slavery in Egypt. The Passover Meal is designed to reenact and remember what took place in Exodus.

The twelve disciples are with Jesus, and they are reclining at a table that is full of all the traditional food for the Passover Seder. Each dish shares an important insight into the story. The unleavened bread is there to remind them that the Israelite slaves had to leave Egypt quickly, and they didn't have enough time to wait around for the dough to rise. The bitter herbs and horseradish are there to remind them of the bitterness and harshness of slavery. The green vegetables dipped into salt water are there to remind them of the tears and sweat of the slaves back in Egypt. On the table there is also four cups of wine, symbolizing the four expressions of deliverance promised by Almighty God in the Exodus story:

Say therefore to the Israelites, 'I am the Lord, and I will free you from the burdens of the Egyptians and deliver you from slavery to them. I will redeem you with an outstretched arm and with mighty acts of judgment. I will take you as my people, and I will be your God. You shall know that I am the Lord your God, who has freed you from the burdens of the Egyptians.

(Exodus 6:6, 7)

The four promises found within this text state: "I will free you; I will deliver you; I will redeem you; and I will take you." The first cup speaks to God's promise of freeing the Israelites from the burdens of the Egyptians. The second cup speaks to God's promise of delivering the Israelites from slavery. The third cup speaks to God's promise of redeeming the Israelites (This cup was not consumed. It was poured out in preparation for Elijah's coming before the Messiah). The fourth cup speaks to God's covenantal relationship with the Israelites.

The primary dish on the table, at the very center, is a lamb that had been sacrificed at the Temple by the priests. The Passover lamb, or the Paschal lamb as it is often called, symbolizes when the angel of death entered the land of Egypt (we discussed this in chapter one). The angel of death killed every first-born child, but the angel passed over those who had placed the sacrificial blood of a lamb on their door posts. The Israelites who followed God's instruction were spared. This is the defining story of the Jewish people, and this is what Jesus, and his disciples, are celebrating.

Dinner Drama

Like most family style dinners, there is an element of drama involved. Most families usually have one person around the dinner table at Thanksgiving or Christmas who is determined to cause a scene. The Passover Supper is no exception.

Jesus is troubled because he knows that he will soon enter deep suffering and even death. In just a short time, Jesus will be arrested, put on trial, beaten, mocked, and crucified.

To make matters worse, someone is going to betray Jesus – someone who is considered to be a very close friend. Jesus turns to his twelve disciples and says, "Truly I tell you, one of you will betray me, one who is eating with me" (Mark 14:18).

When the disciples hear this, they are completely shocked. The disciples had given up everything to follow Jesus. Besides, only four days earlier the crowds were waving palm branches and singing his praises as he entered Jerusalem. This just doesn't make any sense.

"How could this be?" they probably think to themselves. "How could one of us, one of the Twelve, betray Jesus? After all, we are his biggest fans. We are the ones who have supported his ministry. We are a part of his inner circle. Which one of us could possibly betray him?"

They look around at one another, trying to identify the culprit, but they are unable to do this just by looking. You get the sense that each one of the disciples begin to experience some self-doubt as they take turns going around the room asking, "Surely not I, Lord?" (Mark 14:19). In their fear and doubt they think to themselves, "It couldn't possibly be me, could it?"

Jesus knew all of this was coming. He had foretold of his death three times already. At the table, among his friends, Jesus identifies his betrayer, saying:

> *"It is one of the twelve, one who is dipping bread into the bowl with me. For the Son of Man goes as it is written of him, but woe to that one by whom the Son of Man is betrayed! It would have been better for that one not to have been born."*
>
> *(Mark 14:20, 21)*

Before the night is over, Judas will betray Jesus by handing him over to the Sanhedrin. Hearing about how Jesus will be betrayed is disconcerting, unnerving, and discomfiting. It's difficult to image Jesus being betrayed by his closest friend.

The Shock of Betrayal

In one of his most famous plays *Julius Caesar*, William Shakespeare tells a story about the betrayal of a friend. It is tragic that Julius Caesar's death comes at the hands of his best friend, Brutus. As the knife is plunged into his back, Caesar cries out, "*Et tu, Brute*," or "You too, Brutus?"[23]

By saying this, Caesar is essentially saying, "I expected this from others, but I never expected this from you. How could you do this to me?" It is as if the pain of the knife paled in comparison to the pain of betrayal from his friend.

It is easy for us to look back and think, "Oh, of course it's Judas. It is so obvious that Judas is the one who will betray Jesus." The disciples, however, give no indication of knowing this. They never say, "Oh, yeah, that makes sense. Judas was always an outcast. He was the only one that was from a big city. Not only that, but he was the one who looked after our money. He never really fit in. He showed all the sings of mental illness. He was a bad apple from the very start. Of course, he would be the one to stab Jesus in the back."

Even with Jesus' warning, the other disciples don't see this coming. They are completely shocked at the possibility of one of their own betraying Jesus. After all, the disciples have walked with Jesus over the past three years. They have watched Jesus heal the sick and cast out many demons. They have watched him heal lepers, debate religious leaders, and teach with incredible authority. They have watched him calm storms, walk on water, feed thousands of people, and they have even seen him raise the dead! These twelve men have spent countless hours with him—talking to him, learning from him, and following him. How could one of the Twelve betray Jesus?

It would be easier for us if we could paint Judas Iscariot as an evil and horrible human being. It would be better if Judas had shown some signs of bad behavior. It would be better if the disciples could have seen this coming and kept an eye on him, but only Jesus knew what was going on with Judas. Only Jesus himself could foresee this happening.

Perhaps you have experienced a sense of betrayal in your own life. Perhaps someone spread untrue gossip behind your back. Or maybe someone whom you trusted shared personal information with others and betrayed your confidence. Or maybe a loved one became unfaithful and broke your trust. Perhaps you know what it feels like to be betrayed, to feel like you can no longer trust someone that you once cared for, loved, and trusted.

Experiencing a painful betrayal can make it difficult to move forward. The pain and vulnerability that affected Jesus speaks to us as well. We can find solace and comfort knowing that we are not alone in our pain, because Christ knows what it is like to feel betrayed.

The difficult truth, however, is that we are sometimes the ones who do the betraying. If we are being honest with ourselves, we may be left with the realization that we sometimes live out the role of Judas Iscariot. As the Reverend Nancy Mikoski states:

Maybe the ones who betray us are not the demons we imagine them to be. Those who would betray are a lot more like you and me. It is easy to look down our noses at Judas and imagine us among the other eleven disciples. As painful as it is, we must admit that we also are capable of betraying those we love, including our Lord.[24]

We, as humans, often want to point to the most extreme examples of evil and try to dismiss the more ordinary, but very real, examples of evil in our own lives. We may not be as guilty as Judas, but that does not mean that we have not caused harm to others.

The season of Lent is a time where we are invited to investigate the depths of our souls. Lent is designed to be a time for us to consider when we have fallen short of being the people that Christ has called us to be. It is the perfect time for us to reflect on our lives and ask a few questions of ourselves. When have we been like Judas? When have we betrayed Jesus? When have we denied Jesus?

The truth is, we have all acted as the betrayer. We have all, in some ways, turned our back on Jesus' call to love God and neighbor. We have all fallen short of living the life that God has called us to live. We have all betrayed Jesus, and our neighbors, at some point in our lives. The good news, however, is that despite our sins, mistakes, betrayals, and shortcomings, Jesus still invites us to join him at the table.

Eucharistic Action

During the Passover Celebration, amid all the drama, Jesus takes the opportunity to do something new and unexpected, by transforming the Seder meal into a sacrament. Jesus takes an old traditional meal and completely transforms it into something new.

There are a few names that we use for this special meal. The first title used for this meal is *Holy Communion* which speaks to the communal aspect of this meal. The second term used is the *Lord's Supper,* or the *Last Supper* which recounts Jesus' time with his disciples during this meal. Finally, the third name used is the term *Eucharist* which means "thanksgiving."

The Last Supper is overflowing with what some scholars call, "Eucharistic Action." There is taking, thankful blessing, breaking, giving, eating, and remembering.[25]

First, Jesus *takes bread.* The bread represents nourishment and survival. Bread is something that has become so ingrained in our everyday lives that sometimes we take it for granted, but we need bread to survive. Jesus takes this ordinary object that we use every day and turns it into a symbol of something special, a sacrament. The bread becomes an outward and visible sign of an inward and spiritual grace.

Then Jesus *gives thanks for the bread.* Jesus offers a word of thanks to God for the gift of bread that is provided for them. Then, Jesus *breaks the bread,* and when he does this, he simultaneously breaks the news of his upcoming death. The loaf of bread that he rips apart represents his body which will also be broken. Then, he *gives the bread* to his disciples and says, "Take; this is my body" (Mark 14:22). He gives the bread as he gives of himself.

Likewise, after the supper, Jesus takes a cup of wine. In the same fashion he gives thanks for it and gives it to his disciples, saying:

> *"This is my blood of the covenant, which is poured out for many. Truly I tell you, I will never again drink of the fruit of the vine until that day when I drink it new in the kingdom of God."*
>
> *(Mark 14:24, 25)*

As Jesus offers a new cup, a fifth cup, he also offers a new promise. The fifth cup of wine symbolizes God's promise of deliverance through the blood of the covenant in Jesus Christ. In this promise, all of humanity is invited into the kingdom of God.

The Lord's Supper is truly brimming with the eucharistic action of taking, thankful blessing, breaking, giving, eating, and remembering. When we are given Holy Communion, we are invited to share in each of these steps as we actively participate at the table of the Lord.

The bread and the wine are transformed as symbols of Christ's body and blood. As the early Christians would gather, they would share in this time of remembrance. They would take bread, bless it, break it, eat it, and remember Christ's body which was given for us all. When Jesus offers the bread and wine to his disciples, he isn't just feeding them physically, but he is also feeding them spiritually.

As we reflect on this meal, and on the eucharistic action, how might we be inspired to take action? How might this meal invite us to offer bread to the hungry? How might this meal invite us to offer companionship to the lonely? How might this meal invite us to offer forgiveness to those who have betrayed us? How might this meal invite us to enter a deeper relationship with the God who created us in God's own image?

Jesus invites us to come and dine with him, and he tells us that we all have a place at the table. Jesus knows us by name, and we are invited to share in fellowship as we feast on the bread and wine. The sacrament of Holy Communion is a way for the church to fellowship together as a community of believers, to commune with each other and with Christ himself.

When we celebrate communion, we are not only remembering what Christ has done in the past, but we are also invited to commune with the presence of Christ which is with us right here and right now. When we go to the table, Christ's real spiritual presence is with us. Christ is sitting next to us as we dine at his table.

Open Table

The founder of the Methodist Movement, John Wesley, said that we should take communion as often as possible. In fact, he wrote a sermon entitled, "The Duty of Constant Communion." In his sermon, Wesley argues that it is the "duty of every Christian to receive the Lord's Supper as often as he (or she) can"[26] Wesley practiced this in his own life by receiving communion a couple times a week, at least.

One of the things I most appreciate about being an ordained elder in the United Methodist Church is that we celebrate an open table. In other words, one does not have to be a member of the United Methodist Church, or any other church, to receive the elements of bread and wine during Holy Communion. As the "The Great Thanksgiving" states:

"Christ our Lord invites to his table all who love him, who earnestly repent of their sin and seek to live in peace with one another."[27]

Throughout his ministry, Jesus eats with people from all walks of life, and he invites us to join his table as well.

No matter who you are, where you are from, or what you have done, you are invited to share in the feast, to commune with Christ and one another. After all, Holy Communion transcends every barrier including class, ethnicity, theology, and yes, even politics. We all come from different places and have different backgrounds, but Jesus invites us all to come and eat with him. We are all equal at the Table.

The inclusiveness of Jesus' table leads us to ask an important question. Who is at your table? Better yet, who is *not* at your table that should be? Who can you reach out to and invite to come alongside you? How might you practice an open table?

Peter's Denial Foretold

Judas will not be the only one to betray Jesus. Following the Last Supper, Jesus breaks more bad news to the disciples. Jesus tells them that they will all desert him and abandon him in his time of need.

Peter hears Jesus say this, and he is indignant. He says, "Even though all become deserters, I will not" (Mark 14:29). Jesus responds, "Truly I tell you, this day, this very night, before the cock crows twice, you will deny me three times" (Mark 14:30). But Peter is insistent. Peter says, "Even though I must die with you, I will not deny you" (Mark 14:31), and all the disciples say the same thing.

Before we are too hard on the disciples, let us be honest about our own lives. There are times when we have not loved God with our whole heart. When we have failed to be an obedient church. When we have not done God's will. When we have broken God's law. When we have rebelled against God's love. When we have not loved our neighbors. When we have not heard the cry of the needy.[28] When we have acted as the betrayer.

Even so, as we journey closer to the cross, as we look upon Jesus, as we join in with the crowd as and shout, "Crucify him," as we mock and turn away, Jesus still makes room for us at the table. In the act of Holy Communion, Jesus foretells of his crucifixion, and he offers himself up as a sacrifice in order to restore us into right relationship with God.

Over the next few hours, Judas Iscariot will betray Jesus with a kiss in exchange for a few silver coins. Peter will deny Christ three times before the cock crows. The disciples will desert Jesus, right after falling asleep in his hour of need. And yet, Jesus still shares in this meal with them. Jesus offers the bread and wine to all the disciples, Judas included. In this act, we find hope knowing that Christ's love surpasses all our sins, mistakes, and failures. No matter who we are or what we have done, we are all invited to sit at the table with Jesus.

Prayer

Communal God, we remember your Son's Last Supper with his disciples in the Upper Room. We remember how Jesus invited them to take part in Eucharistic Action. Help us to embrace this meal and to take action in our own lives. Thank you for inviting us all to the table, and may we also be willing to share in communion with Christ and one another. O God, give us the strength and courage to make the necessary changes in our lives. Allow us to follow Jesus as he journeys closer and closer to the cross; and allow us to receive him as the king of our lives. For we ask all these things in Jesus' name. Amen.

Reflection Questions

1. Sharing in meals together is an important aspect of human connection. Do you have a favorite meal that you enjoy eating during the holidays?

2. Eucharist is another word for communion which means "thanksgiving." Who are you thankful for in your life? What are you thankful for in your life?

3. Sometimes people refrain from receiving communion during worship due to a sense of their own unworthiness to participate. Have you ever struggled with feeling unworthy when receiving Holy Communion? If so, why?

4. The Passover Festival reminded God's people about how God brought them out of slavery in Egypt. God was faithful in delivering God's people. What might the promise in the Lord's Supper bring about deliverance in your life?

5. Judas betrays Jesus, Peter denies Jesus, and the disciples abandon Jesus. When have we been like Judas? When have we been like Peter and the disciples? When have we betrayed Jesus? When have we denied Jesus?

CHAPTER SIX

JESUS IN
THE GARDEN

They went to a place called Gethsemane; and he said to his disciples, "Sit here while I pray." He took with him Peter and James and John, and began to be distressed and agitated. And he said to them, "I am deeply grieved, even to death; remain here, and keep awake." And going a little farther, he threw himself on the ground and prayed that, if it were possible, the hour might pass from him. He said, "Abba, Father, for you all things are possible; remove this cup from me; yet, not what I want, but what you want." He came and found them sleeping; and he said to Peter, "Simon, are you asleep? Could you not keep awake one hour? Keep awake and pray that you may not come into the time of trial; the spirit indeed is willing, but the flesh is weak." And again he went away and prayed, saying the same words. And once more he came and found them sleeping, for their eyes were very heavy; and they did not know what to say to him. He came a third time and said to them, "Are you still sleeping and taking your rest? Enough! The hour has come; the Son of Man is betrayed into the hands of sinners. Get up, let us be going. See, my betrayer is at hand."

Immediately, while he was still speaking, Judas, one of the twelve, arrived; and with him there was a crowd with swords and clubs, from the chief priests, the scribes, and the elders. Now the betrayer had given them a sign, saying, "The one I will kiss is the man; arrest him and lead him away under guard." So when he came, he went up to him at once and said, "Rabbi!" and kissed him. Then they laid hands on him and arrested him. But one of those who stood near drew his sword and struck the slave of the high priest, cutting off his ear. Then Jesus said to them, "Have you come out with swords and clubs to arrest me as though I were a bandit? Day after day I was with you in the temple teaching, and you did not arrest me. But let the scriptures be fulfilled." All of them deserted him and fled. A certain young man was following him, wearing nothing but a linen cloth. They caught hold of him, but he left the linen cloth and ran off naked.

(Mark 14:32-52)

Following the Last Supper, Jesus and eleven of his disciples (by this point Judas has already left to betray Jesus) travel the road that goes through the Kidron Valley, also known as the "Valley of Jehoshaphat," one of the main graveyards in Israel.

Walking through this burial ground is surely an omen for Jesus as he draws closer and closer to his death. This location not only points to Jesus' crucifixion, but it also points to the final judgment where Jesus will judge both the living and the dead. The prophet Joel had even identified this site as the location where the Last Judgement will take place:

"Let the nations rouse themselves, and come up to the valley of Jehoshaphat; for there I will sit to judge all the neighboring nations"

(Joel 3:12)

In this chapter we will journey with Jesus as he agonizes in the Garden of Gethsemane, is betrayed by Judas, and is arrested by the soldiers of the chief priest.

Agonizing in the Garden

Jesus and eleven of his disciples make their way up the Mount of Olives to Gethsemane. The word *Gethsemane* means "oil press" in Aramaic, and it is believed there was an oil press in this location.[29] Mark's Gospel simply refers to this place as Gethsemane, and only John's Gospel refers to it being in a garden (John 18:1). Gethsemane sits at the base of the Mount of Olives, and it is full of olive trees. Amazingly, some of these olive trees that were there during the time of Jesus still remain today. How incredible it must be to look at the same tree and witness the same environment that Jesus himself experienced as a human being!

In the garden, Jesus tells eight of his disciples to sit there while he goes off to pray. Meanwhile, Jesus takes Peter, James, and John with him as they go deeper into the garden. As they walk, Jesus begins to feel more distressed and more agitated. He turns to his three closest disciples and says, "I am deeply grieved, even to death; remain here, and keep awake" (Mark 14:34).

Jesus makes this simple request to his closest friends. He leans on these three disciples that have been with him for the past three years, reaching out for prayer in his greatest hour of need. Then, he goes further into the garden, throws himself on the ground, and begins to pray,

> *"Abba, Father, for you all things are possible; remove this cup from me; yet, not what I want, but what you want"*
>
> *(Mark 14:36)*

The cup that Jesus speaks about represents real pain, real suffering, and a real death that will take place. The cup represents the sins of the world, a bitter drink that Jesus must swallow.

In this moment, Jesus is experiencing an extreme amount of anxiety and fear as he draws closer to the cross. In fact, Jesus is in so much anguish that Luke's Gospel tells us that "his sweat became like great drops of blood falling down on the ground" (Luke 22:44).

Sweating drops of blood comes from a real-life condition known as *hematohidrosis*. According to experts, hematohidrosis is a very rare medical condition that may occur in an individual who is experiencing extreme levels of stress, strain, or exertion.[30]

Jesus is experiencing so much stress that he is literally sweating drops of blood as he agonizes the fate that awaits him. Seeing Jesus experiencing this amount of anxiety and fear shows us that Jesus knows what we are going through when we experience anxiety and fear in our own lives. Jesus knows what it is like to agonize and suffer over a difficult situation.

Perhaps there have been times in your own life when you have felt like you have more going on than you can handle. Perhaps you have experienced a deep sense of anxiety, stress, fear, and depression. In the Garden of Gethsemane, Jesus is experiencing all these feelings. When we are in a dark place in our own lives, we can know that Jesus relates to our feelings. Jesus is there with us in our most difficult moments. Jesus knows what it is like to go through a difficult and traumatic time.

Following God's Will

Jesus knows what will take place. Jesus has predicted this death three times in Mark's Gospel (Mark 8:31; 9:31; 10:32-34). Nevertheless, he still prays this prayer, asking for God to take his cup of suffering away from him. He knows this will be challenging. Jesus does not want to experience the crucifixion, the excruciating pain, and the humiliation. So, Jesus offers up this prayer to see if there is any other way.

Jesus feels all these emotions, but he still prays for God's will to be done. He says, "Not what I want but what you want" (Mark 14:26). This is an incredibly powerful prayer as Jesus submits his authority over to God the Father. Ultimately, Jesus is willing to go to his death on the cross.

God does not intervene. Instead, God allows Jesus, God's only Son, to go to the cross. For that reason, we might be tempted to think that Jesus' suffering and dying on the cross is truly the will of God. Is it really God's will for Jesus, the Son of God, to die an agonizing death at the hands of humanity? Is this something that God wanted to happen? Of course not!

Just because something happens does not mean that it is the will of God. The pain and crucifixion of Jesus is not something God wanted to inflict upon him. Instead, this is something that humanity did to God's Son.

The pain that we experience in this life does not come from God punishing us or bringing bad things upon us. Instead, it most often comes from what we humans do to one another. The pain and suffering that we experience comes from when we fail to do what God has called us to do. It comes from when we fail to follow God's will for our lives. It comes from others who fail to follow God's will for their lives. It comes from living in a fallen and broken world. This isn't the will of God, but it is an example of our human brokenness. This is reason why Jesus came to live and dwell among us in the first place.

God does not bring about suffering for God's children; however, suffering is still a part of the human experience. Even though God is good and wants the best for us, we still experience suffering. The good news is that God is still with us. God is still present even in the difficult time of life.

Even though Jesus is facing death, he knows that God is present with him. By praying, "Not what I want but what you want" (Mark 14:26), Jesus is being obedient to God's call upon his life. He is willing to do what God is calling him to do even though it is challenging and difficult.

As humans, we sometimes struggle with following God's will for our lives. Sometimes we want to follow our own will, not God's will. We can think of Adam and Eve who were not in the Garden of Gethsemane, but in the Garden of Eden. In that garden, Adam and Eve chose to follow their own will over God's will. God told them,

"You may freely eat of every tree of the garden; but of the tree of the knowledge of good and evil you shall not eat, for in the day that you eat of it you shall die."

(Genesis 2:16, 17)

However, Adam and Eve chose to ignore God's commands and follow their own way instead. The first humans essentially reversed Jesus' Gethsemane prayer. Instead of saying, "not my will but thy will," they said: "not thy will, but my will." Adam and Eve ate from the tree of the knowledge of good and evil. This led to humanity's fall into sin and banishment from the Garden of Eden.

Sometimes we want to follow our will not God's will. Following God's will can often be challenging. It requires us to ask ourselves some difficult questions: How might God be calling you to follow God's will even when it is difficult? How can you put other people's needs above our own? How can you speak up and speak out against injustice? How can you serve others who are in need? How can you take up your crosses and follow Jesus?

John Wesley adapted a prayer from the Puritan tradition that has become known as "The Wesley Covenant Prayer." Praying this prayer gives us the opportunity to ask for God's will to be done in our lives. The prayer says:

I am no longer my own, but thine.
Put me to what thou wilt,
rank me with whom thou wilt.
Put me to doing, put me to suffering.
Let me be employed by thee or laid aside for thee,
exalted for thee or brought low for thee.
Let me be full, let me be empty.
Let me have all things, let me have nothing.
I freely and heartily yield all things
to thy pleasure and disposal.
And now, O glorious and blessed God,
Father, Son, and Holy Spirit,
thou art mine, and I am thine. So be it.
And the covenant which I have made on earth,
let it be ratified in heaven. Amen.[31]

Praying this prayer takes some guts, because it invites us into a deeper way of following God. In this prayer we are asking God to be God. We are asking God to do what God wants, not what we want. That takes guts.

We are invited to say this prayer boldly, because this is a prayer that calls us to give up our own way to follow God's way. It is a prayer that forces us to get our own wants and desires out of the way so that we can focus on our God who can do all things. What would it look like if we were to live out God's will for our lives?

Falling Asleep

After Jesus' prayer, he goes back to check in on his disciples. Jesus finds that as he has been praying in anguish, the disciples have been sleeping. In Jesus' greatest moment of need, the disciples are unable stay awake. Jesus is furious and reprimands Simon Peter, saying:

> *"Simon, are you asleep? Could you not keep awake one hour? Keep awake and pray that you may not come into the time of trial; the spirit indeed is willing, but the flesh is weak."*
>
> *(Mark 14:37, 38)*

Jesus then goes back to praying, offering up the same exact prayer as before, but twice Jesus returns to his disciples and finds them asleep both times. The disciples fail Jesus three times in a row. They fail to do the one thing that Jesus asks of them in his greatest time of need. They are unable to stay awake and be in prayer in his weakest moment.

Before we are too hard on the disciples, we might ask ourselves a few probing questions: How have we failed to be there for our neighbors? When have we fallen short or failed people when they are in a time of need? Are we guilty of sleeping on the job, failing to be the people that God has called us to be?

A Kiss of Betrayal

The third time Jesus returns to his sleeping disciples, Jesus also faces his betrayer. Jesus tells Peter, James, and John:

> *"Are you still sleeping and taking your rest? Enough! The hour has come; the Son of Man is betrayed into the hands of sinners. Get up, let us be going. See, my betrayer is at hand."*

> *(Mark 14:41, 42)*

Judas Iscariot, one of Jesus' own disciples, appears with an entourage of soldiers who are carrying swords and clubs. To mark his betrayal, Judas walks up to Jesus and greets him with a kiss. It is ironic that Judas would greet Jesus in such an affectionate way while at the same time metaphorically stabbing him in the back. Why would Judas do this?

Unfortunately, we do not know Judas' true intentions. Perhaps he was motivated by greed. We know that Judas oversaw the finances as the treasurer. John's Gospel suggests that Judas was a thief and often stole from the treasury (John 12:6). However, Judas only receives 20 pieces of silver in exchange for betraying Jesus (Mark 14:11). This is not a significant amount of money by any means.

On the other hand, perhaps Judas is fed up with Jesus' inaction toward rebelling against the Roman government. Perhaps by betraying Jesus, Judas is trying to force Jesus' hand. Perhaps Judas wants Jesus to be backed into a corner so that he might finally stand up against the oppressive Roman occupation.

We will never know Judas' true intentions, but we do know that Judas goes on to experience guilt and shame after betraying Jesus. After Jesus' arrest, trail, and crucifixion, Judas is so disturbed and distraught that he takes his own life. For this reason, Judas is a very tragic figure in the Passion story. Matthew's Gospel offers a glimpse into Judas' sense of guilt and shame when he tries to return the silver to the chief priests:

Throwing down the pieces of silver in the temple, he departed; and he went and hanged himself. But the chief priests, taking the pieces of silver, said, "It is not lawful to put them into the treasury, since they are blood money." After conferring together, they used them to buy the potter's field as a place to bury foreigners. For this reason that field has been called the Field of Blood to this day.

(Matthew 27:5-8)

The story of Judas is indeed a tragic one, but perhaps there is still good news even for Judas. Maybe Jesus found a way to forgive Judas in the end? Maybe God's grace was extended even to this man who had betrayed the Son of God? After all, this would certainly be in keeping with Jesus' message of love and forgiveness throughout the Gospels. The truth is, we don't know Judas' fate; However, we do know that our God has a reputation of being a forgiving God, and this is very good news for us.

Put Down Your Sword

After Judas kisses Jesus, the soldiers place their hands on Jesus and start to arrest him. In the heat of the moment, one of the disciples draws a sword, hits the servant of the high priest, and cuts off his ear. John's Gospel reports that Simon Peter is the one who wields the sword, and John tells us the servant's name is Malchus (John 18:10). Luke's Gospel goes on to tell us that Jesus reportedly heals Malchus' ear. Jesus touches the man's ear and heals him (Luke 22:51).

Peter is bound and determined to defend Jesus at any cost. He is not willing to idly stand by while Jesus is arrested. He simply must respond, and his impulse is to respond with violence and aggression. In Matthew's Gospel, however, Jesus calls for peace and nonviolence by saying:

> *"Put your sword back into its place; for all who take the sword will perish by the sword. Do you think that I cannot appeal to my Father, and he will at once send me more than twelve legions of angels? But how then would the scriptures be fulfilled, which say it must happen in this way?"*

> *(Matthew 26:52-54)*

Jesus calls Peter to the discipline of nonviolence. Peter's first impulse is to act out of fear, and to violently defend Jesus, but Jesus calls Peter to nonviolence. This is where Jesus calls us as well. Being a peacemaker does not mean that you stand around and do nothing. Instead, being a peacemaker invites us to find ways to respond in love and peace rather than fear and violence. As a peacemaker, Jesus still makes an indictment against those who have come to arrest him saying:

"Have you come out with swords and clubs to arrest me as though I were a bandit? Day after day I was with you in the temple teaching, and you did not arrest me. But let the scriptures be fulfilled."

(Mark 14:48-49)

I wonder if Jesus' complaint made any of the arresting officers hesitate or want to hold back? I wonder if any of them started to question or rethink their decision to arrest this man? I wonder if any of them witnessed Jesus heal Malchus' ear and think—maybe arresting this man is a mistake?

In his sermon "Malchus' Ear: God's Last Love Note to Caiaphas," scholar, professor, and author Dennis F. Kinlaw writes about what might have happened when Malchus went into Caiaphas' office to report about Jesus' arrest. He writes:

"Well, Malchus," Caiaphas demands roughly, "did you get him?"

Malchus hesitates, and then responds quietly as he rubs his right ear, "Yes sir, we got him."

"Did you have any trouble? What about from that big, loud fisherman? Did he cause trouble?"

"Well, yes, sir. He caused a little trouble," replies Malchus, rubbing his ear again, making sure it's still there.

"What was the trouble? Out with it! I want to know what happened."

"Sir, that big fisherman – Peter, they call him – well sir, he sliced off my ear."

Caiaphas stares at Malchus' ear. "Your ear looks okay to me."

"Sir, that's the problem." Says Malchus, "Are you sure we want to arrest HIM?"[32]

Even after the miraculous healing of Malchus' ear, Caiaphas moves forward with his plan. Just as Jesus predicted, his disciples all run away and abandon him. They leave him as he is arrested and led away to go on trial before the religious leaders.

The Naked Young Man

At the end of the arrest scene, there is an unidentified young man who is following Jesus, wearing nothing but a linen cloth. When the soldiers try to grab ahold of him, he runs off completely naked leaving the linen cloth behind. There is a lot of speculation about who this mysterious young man might be.

Could it be a disciple? It's possible that one of Jesus' disciples might be hanging back in the shadows, watching these events unfold. Maybe it was James, John, or even Lazarus of Bethany?

Could it be John Mark, the author of the Gospel of Mark? Perhaps, in this moment, Mark is placing himself in the narrative to insert himself into the story.

Or could it be us? Perhaps Mark's Gospel is inviting us to enter the narrative ourselves. What might we do if we were in the garden of Gethsemane during Jesus' arrest? When have we been naked, vulnerable, and in need of a Savior in our own lives? During this Lenten season, we are invited to enter the Passion narrative with Jesus. We are invited to jump into the story of the Gospels and walk with Jesus as we journey together to the cross.

Prayer

O God, we remember your Son's journey to the Garden of Gethsemane. We remember how Jesus agonized over the difficult road that awaited him. And yet, Jesus prayed, "Not my will but Thy be done." Help us to pray that same prayer. Help us follow you during this Lenten season as we seek to grow closer and closer to you. O God, give us the strength and courage to make the necessary changes in our lives. Allow us to follow Jesus as he journeys closer and closer to the cross; and allow us to receive him as the king of our lives. For we ask all these things in Jesus' name. Amen.

Reflection Questions

1. In the garden Jesus prayed, "Not my will but thy will." In what ways do you choose to follow God's will rather than your own will?

2. Jesus is in aguish as he prays about his cup of suffering. Sometimes following God's will is difficult and challenging. Has following God's will in your own life ever caused you to sacrifice something? Was it worth it?

3. Judas betrays Jesus with a kiss. Have you ever been betrayed by someone close to you? Have you ever betrayed a close friend? Were you able to find forgiveness or reconciliation?

4. Peter responds with violence by attacking Malchus and cutting off his ear. Have you ever experienced a time in your life when you meant well, but you were not truly living up to the standard of what God was calling you to do?

5. When Jesus is arrested, the disciples run in fear. Has the experience of fear ever caused you to run away from something, or someone, in a time of need? How might fear hold you back from living out your Christian life?

~

CHAPTER SEVEN

JESUS
ON TRIAL

They took Jesus to the high priest; and all the chief priests, the elders, and the scribes were assembled. Peter had followed him at a distance, right into the courtyard of the high priest; and he was sitting with the guards, warming himself at the fire. Now the chief priests and the whole council were looking for testimony against Jesus to put him to death; but they found none. For many gave false testimony against him, and their testimony did not agree. Some stood up and gave false testimony against him, saying, "We heard him say, 'I will destroy this temple that is made with hands, and in three days I will build another, not made with hands.'" But even on this point their testimony did not agree. Then the high priest stood up before them and asked Jesus, "Have you no answer? What is it that they testify against you?" But he was silent and did not answer. Again the high priest asked him, "Are you the Messiah, the Son of the Blessed One?" Jesus said, "I am;

> *and 'you will see the Son of Man*
> *seated at the right hand of the Power,'*
> *and 'coming with the clouds of heaven.'"*

Then the high priest tore his clothes and said, "Why do we still need witnesses? You have heard his blasphemy! What is your decision?" All of them condemned him as deserving death. Some began to spit on him, to blindfold him, and to strike him, saying to him, "Prophesy!" The guards also took him over and beat him.

While Peter was below in the courtyard, one of the servant-girls of the high priest came by. When she saw Peter warming himself, she stared at him and said, "You also were with Jesus, the man from Nazareth." But he denied it, saying, "I do not know or understand what you are talking about." And he went out into the forecourt. Then the cock crowed. And the servant-girl, on seeing him, began again to say to the bystanders, "This man is one of them." But again he denied it. Then after a little while the bystanders again said to Peter, "Certainly you are one of them; for you are a Galilean." But he began to curse, and he swore an oath, "I do not know this man you are talking about."

At that moment the cock crowed for the second time. Then Peter remembered that Jesus had said to him, "Before the cock crows twice, you will deny me three times." And he broke down and wept.

(Mark 14:53-72)

Jesus is arrested and transported in the middle of the night, under the cover of darkness. He is brought to the upper city where he arrives at the home of Caiaphas the high priest. Peter follows behind Jesus from a safe distance. He walks into the courtyard, sits among the guards, and warms himself by the fire.

The Sanhedrin, or the Jewish ruling council, is comprised of seventy-one Jewish men who are leaders and elders in the community. They are gathered, at this late hour, to find testimony against Jesus so that they might put him to death.

The only problem is, they can't find adequate testimony to convict Jesus.

People are giving false testimonies that are conflicting and do not agree. Some of the testifiers make false claims saying, "We heard him say, 'I will destroy this temple that is made with hands, and in three days I will build another, not made with hands'" (Mark 14:58).

Even this testimony about Jesus rebuilding the temple conflicts with other reports. There is no testimony or evidence that can convict Jesus of any wrongful behavior. This trial is nothing more than a political stunt, and there is absolutely nothing to charge Jesus with; but this doesn't stop the Council from trying anyway.

Jesus Before the Council

The religious leaders turn their line of questioning away from the testimony of others and directly to Jesus himself. Because the Council is unable to find two or three witnesses who agree with each other, the high priest asks Jesus to address those testifying against him. This is an opportunity for Jesus to either defend himself or offer a confession; but Jesus remains silent.

The high priest gets straight to the heart of the matter and asks Jesus a direct question about his identity. The high priest stands up and asks Jesus, point blank, "Are you the Messiah, the Son of the Blessed One?" (Mark 14:61).

This time Jesus does not remain silent, he speaks up. It is almost like he has been waiting to be asked this specific question. Without any hesitation, Jesus responds, "I am; and 'you will see the Son of Man seated at the right hand of the

Power,' and 'coming with the clouds of heaven'" (Mark 14:62).

The phrase "I am" recalls the story of Moses and the burning bush. In the Book of Exodus, God calls Moses to free the Israelites from slavery in Egypt. God tells Moses that God himself has seen the misery of the Israelites in Egypt and is aware of their pain and suffering. God has heard them crying and is concerned about their suffering. When Moses asks about God's name, God answers, "I AM WHO I AM" (Exodus 3:14). Out of a burning bush, God reveals that God is indeed the source of life itself. God has always been, and God will always be—God is eternal and everlasting.

Jesus embraces this "I am" statement by living into this identity of the same God who called Moses from the burning bush. In the Gospel of John, Jesus takes the phrase "I am" and applies it to himself seven different times. Jesus proclaims the "I am" statements, saying:

I am the bread of life (John 6:35).

I am the light of the world (John 8:12)

I am the gate for the sheep (John 10:9).

I am the good shepherd (John 10:11).

I am the resurrection and the life (John 11:25).

I am the way, the truth, and the life (John 14:6).

I am the true vine (John 15:1).

In the "I am" statements, Jesus draws a direct connection to the God of the universe. In fact, the Gospel of John makes this connection from the very beginning:

In the beginning was the Word, and the Word was with God, and the Word was God. He was in the beginning with God. All things came into being through him, and without him not one thing came into being. What has come into being in him was life, and the life was the light of all people.

(John 1:1-4)

In his trial with the Sanhedrin, Jesus once again identifies himself with the God who proclaims: "I Am Who I Am" (Exodus 3:14). In this statement, Jesus reveals his true identity as the Son of God, the Blessed One, and the Messiah. This is exactly what the religious leaders wanted to hear because Jesus is making a confession that ultimately leads to his crucifixion. Jesus willingly walks right into their trap. The high priest tears his clothes and accuses Jesus of blasphemy. The Council bands together and calls for Jesus' death. This confession is enough to stoke the fire, and it moves Jesus even closer to the cross.

Guilty or Innocent

Jesus is not the first to be falsely accused, and he won't be the last. In her award-winning book *To Kill a Mockingbird*, Harper Lee writes about an innocent man who is wrongfully convicted.

The books tell the story of Tom Robinson, a black man who has been accused of raping a white woman in the fictional town of Maycomb, Alabama. Atticus Finch, a local white attorney, agrees to defend Robinson despite the disapproval and dismay of the white community.

During the trial Atticus provides overwhelming evidence that Robinson's accusers, Mayella Ewell and her father, Bob, are providing false testimony. The truth is that Mayella and Robinson engaged in a consensual relationship. However, when the pair was caught by Mayella's father, she accused Robinson of raping her so that she could avoid her father's wrath.

Despite the clear evidence proving Robinson's innocence, the all-white jury convicts him anyway. When Robinson tries to escape prison, he is shot and killed. In response to Robinson's conviction, Atticus tells his two children, Jem and Scout:

The one place where a man ought to get a square deal is in a courtroom, be he any color of the rainbow, but people have a way of carrying their resentments right into a jury box.[33]

It is believed that Harper Lee based her novel on several actual trials that convicted black men of violent crimes in the deep south. Harper Lee's own father was an attorney named A.C. Lee who defended a black father and son, Frank and Brown Ezell, who were accused of murder. They were found guilty and were executed by hanging. Following this trial A.C. Lee never took on another criminal case again.[34]

It is speculated that Lee's novel was also influenced by the Scottsboro Boys trial. In 1931, a group of white teenagers accused black teenagers of starting a fight on a train in Alabama. In addition, two white women accused some of the black teens of raping them. The cases were rushed through the legal system and the accused had very poor legal representation. The all-white jury convicted all but one of the defendants.[35]

The Scottsboro Boys case eventually made its way to the U.S. Supreme Court where the charges against four of the defendants were dropped. The rest of the defendants either escaped or were released from jail. The one defendant who had received a death sentence went into hiding and eventually received a pardon from the governor. He later wrote a book about his experiences. The Scottsboro Boys trial has become a clear and prime example of injustice that can occur in all-white juries.[36]

Unfortunately, these stories are not isolated incidents. There is a long history of innocent people being wrongfully convicted and sentenced to death.

In his book *Just Mercy*, Bryan Stevenson tells the true story of when he was a young defense attorney who was representing Walter McMillian, a black man who has been wrongfully convicted for murder and was on death row. In the book he discusses the challenges he faced while trying to prove McMillian's innocence through a broken and corrupted system. Stevenson writes:

Scores of innocent people have been exonerated after being sentenced to death and nearly executed. Hundreds more have been released after being proved innocent of noncapital crimes through DNA testing. Presumptions of guilt, poverty, racial bias, and a host of other social, structural, and political dynamics have created a system that is defined by error, a system in which thousands of innocent people now suffer in prison.[37]

Life is a precious gift from God, but we forget that sometimes. If Jesus was wrongfully convicted and sentenced to death, how should Christians feel about others who are wrongfully convicted and put on death row? To put it another way: What would Jesus say about capital punishment? If Jesus were around today, would he support the death penalty?

The Way of Peace

In the previous chapter we discussed Jesus' response to Peter's violent outburst against Malchus. Jesus calls Peter to lay down his weapon in pursuit of peace. Peter's first impulse was to act out of fear and violently defend Jesus, but Jesus calls Peter to nonviolence. In fact, during his Sermon on the Mount Jesus says, "Blessed are the peacemakers, for they will be called children of God" (Matthew 5:9).

Another example of Jesus' response to violence is found in the Gospel of John. A woman who has been caught in the act of adultery is brought to Jesus. The religious leaders tell Jesus, "Teacher, this woman was caught in the very act of committing adultery" (John 8:4).

The Torah clearly states that the punishment for adultery is death by stoning (Deuteronomy 22:22). Everyone in the crowd already has a stone in their hand, and they are ready to kill this woman. After all, that is how the law has been carried out for generations. And the Pharisees plan to trick Jesus by asking about his opinion. They say, "Now in the law Moses commanded us to stone such women. Now what do you say?" (John 8:5).

Without a word, Jesus stoops down and begins to draw in dust with his finger. He writes something there in the dust as the Pharisees continue to question him. Then like an artful politician, he stands and says, "Let anyone among you who is without sin be the first to throw a stone at her" (John 8:7). Then he goes right back to drawing in the dirt. One by one the people in the mob, beginning with the elders, leave until finally it is just Jesus and the woman left standing there.

Jesus says, "Woman, where are they? Has no one condemned you?" (John 8:10). It's almost like Jesus has been off in his own little world and when he snaps back into reality, he realizes that everyone has gone. And he sees that his answer to the Pharisees did the trick. The woman responds, "No sir" (John 8:11a). To which Jesus replies, "Neither do I condemn you. Go your way, and from now on do not sin again" (John 8:11b).

Years ago, when I was a teenager, I remember my pastor, preaching on this passage about the woman caught in adultery. During his sermon, my pastor said,

Think of all those people who were crowded around with stones in their hands. Do you think they dropped their stones when they heard Jesus' response? Do you think they dropped their stones when they turned to leave? Or do you think they held on to them, waiting for the next opportunity to cast their stones of judgment?

My pastor went on to say that he thinks those in the crowd probably held on to their stones. He argued that it's harder to offer grace than it is to offer damnation. But what about us? Are we holding on to our stones? Are we carrying them around waiting for an opportunity to arise so that we can throw them?

We are sometimes tempted to throw stones at others, to attack the things and the people that are different than us, and to lash out and condemn anyone who disagrees with us. In his book *Hannah's Child*, professor and theologian, Stanley Hauerwas writes:

I am not by nature nonviolent. It is not a natural stance. But one slow step at a time I tried to learn not to live a life

determined by what I was against. Peace is a deeper reality than violence.[38]

Jesus has the incredible ability to forgive sinful and broken people, even the people that threaten him, betray him, and harm him. He has the incredible ability to offer grace, mercy, and peace even in the most difficult situations. Jesus is even able to forgive someone who would deny him three times.

Peter and the Rooster

Meanwhile, Peter stands helplessly in the crowd from a safe distance as he watches the proceedings of the trial take place. Peter is unable to do anything to save Jesus from the accusations that are being hurled at him. All he can do is watch.

As Peter is warming himself by a charcoal fire, one of the servant-girls of the high priest recognizes him as one of Jesus' disciples. She says, "You also were with Jesus, the man from Nazareth" (Mark 14:67). Peter is quick to deny it, saying, "I do not know or understand what you are talking about" (Mark 14:68).

Then the cock crowed.

Again, the servant girl accused Peter of being one of Jesus' disciples say, "This man is one of them" (Mark 14:69). Again, Peter denies it. Then, a third time Peter is accused of being one of Jesus' followers. And a third time, Peter denies it, cursing, "I do not know this man you are talking about" (Mark 14:71).

Then the cock crowed for the second time.

It is at this very moment when Peter remembers what Jesus had told him, "Before the cock crows twice, you will deny me three times" (Mark 14:72). In the Upper Room, earlier this same night, Jesus told Peter this was going to happen. In the realization that Peter has done the very thing he swore he would never do, Peter leaves, weeping bitterly in complete grief.

The story of Peter's denial invites us to ask ourselves some questions. When have we denied Jesus? When have we failed to live the lives that Christ has called us to live? When have we failed to forgive someone when we ourselves have been forgiven by God? When have we fallen short of living into our role as followers of Christ? We have all experienced feelings of guilt, shame, and conviction because of the mistakes we have made. We have all fallen short, but we can still experience redemption. After all, Peter certainly did.

Peter's Redemption

At the very end of the Gospel of John, Peter finds redemption in Christ. After Jesus is resurrected, he appears to his disciples several times. On one occasion, Jesus appears to Peter and gives him three opportunities to affirm him as the Christ. Jesus asks him a very emotional and vulnerable question, "Simon son of John, do you love me more than these?" (John 21:15a). It is interesting to note that Jesus does not call him by his usual name Peter, but instead Jesus calls him, "Simon son of John." This shows that Jesus means business. Peter replies, "'Yes, Lord; you know that I love you.'" Jesus said to him, 'Feed my lambs'" (John 21:15b).

Jesus repeats the same question again, "Simon son of John, do you love me?" (John 21:16a). Again, Peter replies, "'Yes, Lord; you know that I love you.' Jesus said to him, 'Tend my sheep'" (John 21:16b). A third time Jesus asks him, "Simon son of John, do you love me?" (John 21:17a). At this point, Peter is getting his feelings hurt a little bit. Why would Jesus ask him this same question three times in a row? A confused Peter quickly responds, "'Lord, you know everything; you know that I love you.' Jesus said to him, 'Feed my sheep.'" (John 21:17b).

At first it might seem like Jesus is being a little clingy. He appears desperate to receive Peter's admiration and love, but, in reality, Jesus is cutting through to the heart of the matter.

This threefold question reminds us of Peter's threefold denial. We can flash back to when Peter was standing around a different charcoal fire, and three times he is asked, "Aren't you one of Jesus' disciples?" And three times Peter denies knowing Christ. Three times Peter says, "I do not know him."

Now, in this interaction with Peter, Jesus gives him an opportunity to answer the call to discipleship once again. This threefold question: "Do you love me?" gives Peter three opportunities to answer this call. Jesus gives Peter this opportunity to redeem himself.

Perhaps this is also a call for all disciples, including us. Perhaps Jesus is also asking us the question, "Do you love me?" and if we say "yes," Jesus is quick to remind us that we are called to actually do something about it. During this Lenten season, we are invited to live out Jesus' message of love. How might we offer our love to God and one another by meeting people's needs in our community and in the world? How might we embrace the "I AM" even when we are tempted to deny him?

Prayer

God of Justice, we remember how your Son was put on trial before the Sanhedrin and wrongfully accused. We remember how Jesus revealed his true identity as the Son of Man who has come to bring peace to the world. Help us to embrace Christ's call to peacemaking in our own relationships. May we offer forgiveness to one another, even when it is difficult. O God, give us the strength and courage to make the necessary changes in our lives. Allow us to follow Jesus as he journeys closer and closer to the cross; and allow us to receive him as the king of our lives. For we ask all these things in Jesus' name. Amen.

Reflection Questions

1. Jesus is falsely accused and put on trial. Have you ever been blamed for something that wasn't your fault? How did you handle that situation?

2. Jesus was wrongfully convicted and sentenced to death. How should we, as Christians, feel about the death penalty? Do you think Jesus would support the death penalty?

3. As Christians, we are called to be peacemakers. How can you be an advocate for peacemaking in your own relationships? Who might you need to forgive for this to happen?

4. Peter fulfills Jesus' prophecy by denying him three times. Have you ever denied Christ, either by thought, word, or deed?

5. Peter finds redemption through Christ's call to love and serve. How might you offer love to God and others through meeting people's needs in your community and in the world?

CHAPTER EIGHT

JESUS
AND PILATE

As soon as it was morning, the chief priests held a consultation with the elders and scribes and the whole council. They bound Jesus, led him away, and handed him over to Pilate. Pilate asked him, "Are you the King of the Jews?" He answered him, "You say so." Then the chief priests accused him of many things. Pilate asked him again, "Have you no answer? See how many charges they bring against you." But Jesus made no further reply, so that Pilate was amazed.

Now at the festival he used to release a prisoner for them, anyone for whom they asked. Now a man called Barabbas was in prison with the rebels who had committed murder during the insurrection. So the crowd came and began to ask Pilate to do for them according to his custom. Then he answered them, "Do you want me to release for you the King of the Jews?" For he realized that it was out of jealousy that the chief priests had handed him over. But the chief priests stirred up the crowd to have him release Barabbas for them instead. Pilate spoke to them again, "Then what do you wish me to do with the man you call the King of the Jews?" They shouted back, "Crucify him!" Pilate asked them, "Why, what evil has he done?" But they shouted all the more, "Crucify him!" So Pilate, wishing to satisfy the crowd, released Barabbas for them; and after flogging Jesus, he handed him over to be crucified.

(Mark 15:1-15)

Just after daybreak, early on Friday morning, Jesus is delivered to the home of Pontius Pilate, the fifth Roman governor of the province of Judaea under Emperor Tiberius.

Pilate's home, the Antonia Fortress, is a structure named after Mark Antony and built by Herod the Great. The building was nestled just north of the Temple Mount, because its original purpose was for the protection of the Temple itself.[39] However, during the time of Jesus, the sacred site has been commandeered and is occupied by a Roman military presence. The fact that a holy site would be used for military occupation no doubt angered the Jewish people. Despite this, the religious rulers still seek help from the Roman government in bringing about Jesus' downfall. It is on the courtyard of the Antonia Fortress that Pilate publicly interrogates Jesus.

Jesus and Pilate

Pilate begins, much like the Sanhedrin did, with a question about Jesus' identity. The Sanhedrin asked Jesus, "Are you the Messiah, the Son of the Blessed One?" (Mark 14:61). Likewise, Pilate asks Jesus, "Are you the King of the Jews?" (Mark 15:2a).

In their book *The Last Week: What the Gospels Really Teach About Jesus' Final Days in Jerusalem*, Marcus Borg and John Dominic Crossan address Pilate's tone in this question by writing:

We should probably hear a mocking emphasis on the word
"you" in Pilate's question. "You" – a Jewish peasant, already
beaten, bloodied, and bound, standing powerless before me
– "are you the king of the Jews?"[40]

Jesus is an unlikely candidate to be any sort of king, let
alone the King of the Jews. Jesus is in custody, he is beaten
and bloodied, and he is being treated as a criminal. And yet,
there is something about Jesus that points to the divine.

Jesus answers Pilate's mocking question, "Are you the
king of the Jews?" with an equally mocking answer, "You say
so" (Mark 15:2b). Again, we can hear the mocking emphasis
on the word "you" in Jesus' answer. "You" – a Roman soldier,
arrogant, pompous, standing before me – "you say so."

Jesus' answer is open to interpretation. Perhaps he is
answering in the affirmative, saying that he is indeed the
king of the Jews. Perhaps he is simply saying that he isn't
going to disagree with Pilate. Either way, in his answer,
Jesus alludes to his kingship, but he doesn't elaborate.

This is when the chief priests interject. They throw every
accusation they possibly can at Jesus, hoping something will
stick. Pilate is amazed at Jesus' lack of concern. Amid all the
accusations, Jesus remains silent. In fact, Jesus will not say
another word in the Gospel of Mark until he is hanging on
the cross.

Jesus' silence is remarkable. At first glance it seems like
Jesus is being agnostic or apathetic about his situation; but
in his silence Jesus is embracing his role as the suffering
servant who has come to fulfill God's purpose for humanity.
The prophet Isaiah provides a picture of the suffering
servant that is ultimately fulfilled in Christ. Isaiah says:

He was oppressed, and he was afflicted,
yet he did not open his mouth;
like a lamb that is led to the slaughter,
and like a sheep that before its shearers is silent,
so he did not open his mouth.

(Isaiah 53:7)

In this prophecy, there are some very clear parallels to Jesus. Jesus is oppressed and afflicted, but he remains silent. Jesus accepts his fate and moves forward to fulfill God's purpose.

Back and Forth

In John's Gospel, however, Pilate and Jesus engage in further conversation, going back and forth. Here is their extended conversation:

Then Pilate entered the headquarters again, summoned Jesus, and asked him, "Are you the King of the Jews?" Jesus answered, "Do you ask this on your own, or did others tell you about me?" Pilate replied, "I am not a Jew, am I? Your own nation and the chief priests have handed you over to me. What have you done?" Jesus answered, "My kingdom does not belong to this world. If my kingdom belonged to this world, my followers would be fighting to keep me from being handed over to the Jews. But as it is, my kingdom is not from here." Pilate asked him, "So you are a king?" Jesus answered, "You say that I am a king. For this I was born, and for this I came into the world, to testify to the truth. Everyone who belongs to the truth listens to my voice." mouth.

(John 18:33-37)

In this back-and-forth exchange, Pilate and Jesus discuss Jesus' identity. In their private conversation, Pilate asks Jesus a very straight forward question, "Are you the King of the Jews?" (John 18:33). Pilate is trying to do one simple thing, determine if Jesus is innocent or guilty.

Instead of responding "yes" or "no," Jesus responds by asking Pilate the question, "Do you ask me this on your own, or did others tell you about me?" (John 18:34). Jesus rarely answers a direct question. He almost *always* answers a question with another question. Pilate is at the top of the judicial process. He is the one tasked with interrogating Jesus, but Jesus turns things around on Pilate.

Pilate returns with yet another question, saying, "I am not a Jew, am I? Your own nation and the chief priests have handed you over to me. What have you done?" (John 18:35).

At this point I wish Jesus would say something. I wish he would tell Pilate that he hasn't done anything wrong. He could explain to Pilate that this is all just a big misunderstanding. He could explain to Pilate that he hasn't committed any crimes and that he is innocent. I wish Jesus would perform a miracle to show everyone that he is God's Son. I wish Jesus would prove to Pilate that he truly is the Son of God who has come to save the world, but that is not what Jesus does.

Instead, after these questions go back and forth, Jesus says, "My Kingdom is not from this world. If my kingdom were from this world, my followers would be fighting to keep me from being handed over to the Jews. But as it is, my kingdom is not from here." (John 18:36).

This is an unusual response. Why does Jesus feel the need to refer to his kingdom when he is talking to a man who bows before a king named Caesar?

In this statement, Jesus makes it clear that he poses a threat to the political establishment. By saying this, he is claiming that his kingdom is bigger and better than Caesar's kingdom. This is a controversial statement for Jesus to make considering Caesar was supposed to be the only king.

Pilate hears this response and asks the next logical question. "So you are a king?" (John 18:37a). Jesus responds, "You say that I am a king, and you are right. For this I was born, and for this I came into the world, to testify to the truth. Everyone who belongs to the truth listens to my voice" (John 18:37b). Pilate offers the final response, "What is truth?" (John 18:38).

One can't help but think about when Jesus told his followers, "If you continue in my word, you are truly my disciples, and you will know the truth, and the truth will make you free" (John 8:31, 32). Jesus is the truth, but Jesus is not set free. At least not yet.

Strangely enough, Marks' Gospel tells us that Pilate's interaction with Jesus leads to the release of another prisoner named Barabbas.

Barabbas

It is a tradition that every year during the Passover festival Pontius Pilate releases a prisoner, whoever the people choose, no questions asked. This "get out of jail free card" is not just for the game *Monopoly*. It is also a way for the Roman government to keep control over the Jewish people and avoid an uprising. It is at this point that we are introduced to Barabbas.

Barabbas is as an insurrectionist who led a revolt against the Romans, committed murder, and robbery. Barabbas is a convicted criminal who is imprisoned along with other rebels. There is definitive proof that Barabbas has committed the crimes that he is accused of committing. He is guilty, no question.

Then we have Jesus, an innocent man who is wrongfully convicted. At this point even Pilate realizes that Jesus is innocent and is only on trial because of the jealousy of the religious leaders.

Therefore, Pilate decides that he will offer these two men up, and the crowd can choose which one of them will go free, Jesus or Barabbas. The choice seems clear to Pilate. Surely the crowd will choose Jesus. There is no evidence, no proof, that Jesus has done anything wrong. Be that as it may, the crowd does not choose Jesus. Instead, the crowd selects Barabbas to go free.

Pilate asks, "Then what do you wish me to do with the man you call the King of the Jews?" But the crowd shouts back, "Crucify Him! Crucify Him!"[41]

Mob Mentality

What would cause this type of behavior toward an innocent man who has done nothing wrong? Well, perhaps the religious leaders were egging on the crowd, spreading lies and misinformation about Jesus. Maybe they hired people to go out into the crowd and cause a scene by calling for Jesus' crucifixion. Or perhaps we can chalk this all up to the barbaric nature of the ancient world. Besides, public stonings, crucifixions, and gladiator games (methods of death and execution) were means of entertainment for the people.

The sad truth, however, is that there is not much need for *"The Why"* when it comes to mob mentality. Often, terrible things happen without much reason at all and, unfortunately, mob mentality is all too real in our world today. Mob mentality has been evident in the most horrific events throughout history, such as: the Salem Witch Trials, the Slave Trade, the Holocaust, and the Red Scare. Mob mentality is even in our politics, die hard Republicans and Democrats who condemn the other side no matter the circumstances. It exists on the internet and social media as well. People make up their minds regardless of the facts.

Speak Up, Speak Out

In situations of tension and division, we might find ourselves on one side or the other. Most often, however, we find ourselves in the crowds as bystanders. When we see injustices in our world take place, what do we do? How do we respond? When Russia invades the Ukraine, do we speak up, or do we think that it doesn't really concern us? When we see someone being bullied or picked on, do we step in and intervene? When someone tells a racist joke do we laugh, do we keep quiet, do we say anything?

There are times in our lives when we are bystanders in the crowd. Maybe we are not actively doing anything to hurt anyone, maybe we are not directly causing harm, but are we do anything to stop it from happening?

The film *Hotel Rwanda* is based on a true story about the conflict that occurred between the Hutu and the Tutsi people that caused a genocide in Rwanda. At one point during the movie, a Rwandan man named Paul (played by Don Cheadle) has a conversation with a reporter named Jack (played by Joaquin Phoenix). The conversation is as follows:

> **Paul:** *"I am glad that you have shot this footage and that the world will see it. It is the only way we have a chance that people might intervene."*
>
> **Jack:** *"And if no one intervenes, is it still a good thing to show?"*
>
> **Paul:** *"How can they not intervene when they witness such atrocities?"*
>
> **Jack:** *"I think if people see this footage they'll say, 'Oh my God that's horrible,' and then go on eating their dinners."*[42]

I'm sure there were a lot of people that day who were shouting "Crucify Him" at Jesus; however, I'm also sure there were a lot of people who were bystanders, who were silent, who maybe disagreed. But they said nothing.

There is no one speaking up for Jesus. All of his followers are silent, or they have gone into hiding. His disciples are nowhere to be found. The only person left to advocate for Jesus, is Jesus!

Christ the King

It's ironic because Jesus actually has the power to stop all of this from happening. Jesus himself can prevent his own crucifixion from happening with the snap of his fingers. He can stop it all, right here and right now, but he doesn't. After all, he truly is the King of the Jews and the Son of God.

However, Jesus doesn't operate as the kind of king that most people expect. Jesus does not function like your typical political leader. He isn't interested in being relevant, spectacular, or powerful. Jesus is focused on something much deeper. Jesus came to right our wrongs, but not through playing politics, not through some new piece of legislation, and not through a mandate that was given to him by his voters. Jesus has a much better solution that will last throughout eternity.

Jesus speaks about the kingdom of God where there is peace instead of war, liberation instead of oppression, service instead of invasion, care for the poor instead of entitlement for the rich, generosity instead of greed, and inclusivity instead of exclusion. The kingdom of God turns the whole world upside down.

In the year 1225, Saint Francis of Assisi wrote the hymn, "All Creatures of our God and King." In the first verse we sing:

> *All creatures of our God and King,*
> *Lift up your voice and with us sing*
> *Oh, praise ye! Alleluia!*
> *O brother sun with golden beam.*
> *O sister moon with softer gleam.*
> *Oh, praise ye! Oh, praise ye!*
> *Alleluia! Alleluia! Alleluia!*[43]

Jesus is king, and in this song, even the sun and moon shouts out praises to God our king. In this song, we are reminded that Jesus is the king of the cosmos. Jesus doesn't really seem like the king that we might expect. Jesus isn't extravagantly wealthy. He doesn't seem to have much of any political power. He doesn't live in a palace or in a castle. He doesn't fit the typical bill for a king.

Instead, Jesus laid down his life. Jesus responded with peace and never with violence. The amazing thing is that we serve a King who humbled himself and carried a cross, who loves and cares for us, who offers us grace when we really deserve damnation. We serve a King who bring forth love and light and truth. Jesus is not the King that was expected, but he is the King that we needed.

Appropriate Restraint

Jesus shows his glory *by* going to the cross. He exercises his power *by* showing restraint. Have you ever had power, but chose to exercise restraint instead? That can be a difficult thing to do.

The famous preacher, Fred Craddock, tells a story about restraint. Several years ago, he was asked to preach at the President's prayer breakfast in Seoul, South Korea. The host of the event was a Four-Star General, named Richard Stilwell. Stilwell had gathered his officers and enlisted personnel for the breakfast. During the prayer time, the soldiers prayed for mothers and fathers, for sisters and babies, for wives, girlfriends, and for peace in the world.

Then Fred Craddock said a few words, gave a benediction, and the soldiers were dismissed. He shook hands with the general and thanked him for his gracious hospitality.

General Stilwell said, "Fred, I want you to remember us in prayer."

Fred said, "I will, General. You know I will."

Stilwell continued, "Not for more power, we have the power. In just one afternoon we could destroy this whole place. Pray that we have the appropriate restraint."

What an unusual request, "Pray that we have the appropriate restraint."[44]

Jesus has a consistent message throughout the Gospel narrative. Jesus says, "For those who want to save their life will lose it, and those who lose their life for my sake will find it" (Matthew 16:25). Jesus says, "So the last will be first, and the first will be last" (Matthew 20:16). Jesus says, "All who exalt themselves will be humbled, and all who humble themselves will be exalted" (Matthew 23:12).

Jesus tells us that power, *real power*, is given when we show restraint. Real power is given when we deny ourselves. Real power is given when we serve others. Real power is given when we stop being a bystander and instead take up our crosses and follow Jesus.

Prayer

King Jesus, we remember how you humbled yourself and practiced restraint as you drew closer to the cross. You are a king that we didn't expect, but we are grateful that you are a king better than we could have ever imagined. We thank you that we are allowed to share in the presence of Jesus Christ, the King of kings and the Lord of lords. May we feel connected and loved by the King of the Cosmos, the One who created us all. Allow us to follow Jesus as he journeys closer and closer to the cross; and allow us to receive him as the king of our lives. For we ask all these things in Jesus' name. Amen.

Reflection Questions

1. Pontius Pilate questions Jesus about his true identity. How do you identify Jesus in your own life? Do you consider Jesus to be your king?

2. Pilate put Jesus and Barabbas before the crowd and offered to release one of them. Crowd mentality took over as they called for Barabbas' freedom and Jesus' crucifixion. Have you ever experienced mob mentality take over in a situation? Did you speak out, or did you go along with the crowd?

3. Jesus was not the kind of king that people expected him to be. He humbled himself instead of exalting himself. How might you learn from Jesus' example in your own life?

4. Jesus is the king of the cosmos. How have you experienced Jesus as king of the universe? Is there a special place in nature where you feel connected to Christ?

5. Rather than proving his divine identity to Pilate or the crowd, Jesus practiced restraint. Jesus remained silent as the crowd called for his crucifixion. What are some ways that you have practiced restraint in your own life?

CHAPTER NINE

JESUS
IS CRUCIFIED

It was nine o'clock in the morning when they crucified him. The inscription of the charge against him read, "The King of the Jews." And with him they crucified two bandits, one on his right and one on his left. Those who passed by derided him, shaking their heads and saying, "Aha! You who would destroy the temple and build it in three days, save yourself, and come down from the cross!" In the same way the chief priests, along with the scribes, were also mocking him among themselves and saying, "He saved others; he cannot save himself. Let the Messiah, the King of Israel, come down from the cross now, so that we may see and believe." Those who were crucified with him also taunted him.

When it was noon, darkness came over the whole land until three in the afternoon. At three o'clock Jesus cried out with a loud voice, "Eloi, Eloi, lema sabachthani?" which means, "My God, my God, why have you forsaken me?" When some of the bystanders heard it, they said, "Listen, he is calling for Elijah." And someone ran, filled a sponge with sour wine, put it on a stick, and gave it to him to drink, saying, "Wait, let us see whether Elijah will come to take him down." Then Jesus gave a loud cry and breathed his last. And the curtain of the temple was torn in two, from top to bottom. Now when the centurion,

who stood facing him, saw that in this way he breathed his
last, he said, "Truly this man was God's Son!"

(Mark 15:25-39)

Jesus is at Golgotha – "the place of the Skull" – the site of the crucifixion. Everything in the Gospel story has been leading up to this point. Jesus has finally reached the cross, and it is still a mystery as to how it got to this point. Pilate has found nothing wrong with Jesus. Herod has found nothing wrong with Jesus. Jesus has done nothing wrong.

If Jesus is guilty of anything it's that he preached a message that was too radical, too extreme, and too difficult for people to accept. So, Jesus is crucified. It's easy for us to look back and think how could something like this happen? How could they kill the Son of God?

The hard truth is that if Jesus were here right now preaching that same message, we would probably waste no time sending him right back to the cross. Most likely, we would reject him, ridicule him, and turn our backs on him.

In his darkest moment, the haunting words ring out from the mouth of Jesus, "My God, my God why have you forsaken me?" (Mark 15:34). On the cross Jesus teaches us about the fragile nature of humanity. As Audrey West writes,

Rejected, on the cross, Jesus lives fully into the human experience of bearing the worst that people can inflict on one another. Betrayal, cruelty, suffering: all of it has happened to him.[45]

Jesus proclaims the hard grief of abandonment, suffering in isolation. On the cross, Jesus quotes a powerful and poignant Psalm: "My God, my God, why have you forsaken me?" (Psalm 22:1). This Psalm portrays a dark and hopeless moment of abandonment and fear.

On the cross, Jesus teaches us about what it means to be forsaken. Maybe you have experienced a time in your life when you felt overlooked, ignored, rejected, and forsaken?

The truth is, sometimes we can recognize God's presence among us, and we can feel this strong sense of God moving and working in the different moments of our lives. Often, however, we don't. Often, we are totally unaware of God's presence among us, but just because you might not feel God's presence – doesn't mean that it's not there.

Throughout the Gospel story, it is evident that Jesus is present among us. Jesus is with us even in the mundane and ordinary things of this world. As individuals, we experience the vibrant heart of Jesus beating in us, among us, and through us.

We can relate to Jesus, because he knows what it's like to go through some of the things that we go through as human beings. We can know that Jesus is here with us, even now.

The incredible thing is that Jesus is not only fully human, but Jesus is also fully divine. This means that in our pain and in our suffering, the God of the Universe is here among us. Jesus is at the right hand of the Father, and the Spirit dwells within us.

Take Up Your Cross

Not only does Jesus take up his cross, but he also tells us that his journey to the cross is something that we are called to do as well. Jesus says,

"If any want to become my followers, let them deny themselves and take up their cross daily and follow me. For those who want to save their life will lose it, and those who lose their life for my sake will save it."

(Luke 9:23-24)

This is one of the most difficult teachings that Jesus offers. He invites us to deny ourselves, to give up our own selfish desires, and to take up our crosses and follow him. It is a call to give up our own way of life. It's a call to put aside our own way and follow Jesus' way. Jesus is challenging us to reassess the fundamental way that we live our lives. As Dietrich Bonhoeffer says in his book, *The Cost of Discipleship*:

The cross is not the terrible end of an otherwise God-fearing and happy life, but it meets us at the beginning of our communion with Christ. When Christ calls a man, he bids him come and die.[46]

There is a great radio story from *This American Life* that talks about a four-year-old girl who wanted to know everything there was to know about Jesus. The little girl asked her father to explain who Jesus is to her. The father decided to buy the little girl a children's' Bible.

At night, the father and daughter would read the Bible together. The more the little girl learned about Jesus the more she loved him. Together, they read about Jesus' birth and his teachings.

She would constantly ask her father, "What was that thing Jesus always says?"

Her father would explain to her that it was, "Do onto others as you would have them do unto you."

They would talk about those old words and what they all meant. Then one day they were driving past a big church and out front was an enormous crucifix which showed Jesus stretched out on the cross. The little girl looked at her father and said, "Who's that?"

At that moment, her father realized that he had never really told that part of the story. He realized that he forgot to tell her about the crucifixion and resurrection of Jesus.

He started to explain by saying, "Well, you know, Jesus made a lot of people mad. He made people in the Roman government mad. He made people in the church mad. His message was so difficult, and challenging, and radical that they decided that they had to kill him. They came to the conclusion that he would have to die, because his message was too troublesome."

A few months later, it was mid-January, and the little girl was out of school for Martin Luther King Day. The father took off work that day as well, and they decided to go out to lunch.

They were sitting in a restaurant, and right on the table where they happened to sit down, was the art section of the local newspaper. There, big as life, was a huge drawing by a ten-year-old kid from the local schools of Martin Luther King.

The little girl saw the picture and said, "Who's that?"

Her father said, "Well, as it happens, that's Martin Luther King. He's why you're not in school today. We are celebrating his birthday today."

The little girl said, "So who was he?"

Her father answered, "He was a preacher."

The little girl immediately perked up and said, "Like Jesus?"

The father said, "Yeah, he was, but there was another thing that he was really famous for. He had an important message."

The little girl said, "What was his message?" The father said, "Well, he said that you should treat everybody the same no matter what they look like."

She thought about that for a minute, and she said, "Well that's what Jesus said."

The father answered, "Yeah, I guess it is. You know, I never thought of it that way, but yeah. It is sort of like 'Do onto others as you would have them do unto you.'"

The little girl thought for a minute and looked up and said, "Did they kill him, too?"[47]

The Good News

The cross is a symbol that we see everywhere we look. Whether it be sanded or stained, old or rugged, polished brass or twisted iron. Whether it be on the wall of a church sanctuary, or on a piece of jewelry hanging around someone's neck, or printed on someone's clothing, the cross is the best-known symbol of Christianity. As Thomas à Kempis once wrote:

In the Cross is salvation; in the Cross is life; in the Cross is protection against our enemies; in the Cross is infusion of heavenly sweetness; in the Cross is strength of mind; in the

Cross is joy of spirit; in the Cross is excellence of virtue; in the Cross is perfection of holiness.[48]

It is the cross that directs us to the saving grace of God through Jesus Christ. The cross expresses and symbolizes the divine love of God through the sacrifice of Jesus Christ. Jesus suffered, was crucified, died, and was buried in order to reconcile us to God. As the *Book of Discipline of the United Methodist Church* states:

> *We believe God was in Christ reconciling the world to himself. The offering Christ freely made on the cross is the perfect and sufficient sacrifice for the sins of the whole world, redeeming man from all sin, so that no other satisfaction is required.*[49]

Jesus is here to actively do something about the problem of sin and brokenness that exists between us and God. Jesus has come to put us back in right relationship with God. Jesus has come to enter our lives and deal with our struggles, sins, and mistakes.

In the coming of Jesus, we find redemption. In the coming of Jesus, we find that we are not alone. Jesus is here with us – walking with us, talking to us, guiding us, teaching us, forgiving us, weeping with us, laughing with us, and raising us.

The Centurion

At Jesus' death on the cross, we hear a proclamation from the most unlikely character – a Roman centurion who proclaims, "Truly this man was God's Son!" (Mark 15:39). This centurion is the only human being in the entire Gospel of Mark to refer to Jesus as the Son of God. At the foot of the cross, this centurion says what the crowd is not allowed to say. He says what Jesus' disciples have been unable, or unwilling, to proclaim.

We don't know a lot about him. We aren't given his name, and we don't know what part he played in carrying out Jesus' crucifixion – although, we can be sure that he had a part to play. We can only speculate about what role that might have been. Perhaps the centurion had been involved from the very the beginning of Jesus' Passion story.

For all we know, this centurion could have been one of the soldiers that had arrested Jesus in the Garden of Gethsemane. In the Garden, he would have seen Jesus' disciples flee. He would have seen Simon Peter fighting for Jesus by cutting off Malchus' ear (the servant of the high priest), and he would have also seen Jesus heal Malchus and restore his ear. He would have heard Jesus tell Simon Peter, "Put your sword back into its place; for all who take the sword will perish by the sword" (Matthew 26:25).

For all we know, this centurion could have transported Jesus to all his destinations – to the house of Caiaphas (the high priest), then to Pilate's Palace, then to Herod, then back to Pilate. He could have overheard all the conversations that Jesus had with these rulers and leaders. When Pilate ordered Jesus to be whipped and beaten, this centurion could have been one placed in charge of the beating. He could have joined in with them. He could have been the one who fashioned the crown of thorns and placed it on Jesus' head.

Then, at the crucifixion site, this centurion could have been the one to nail Jesus' hands and feet to the cross. For all we know, this centurion could have witnessed and participated in every aspect of Jesus' journey to the cross.

But one thing we do know for certain is that he was there, he was present, he was a witness to Jesus' actual death on that Friday.

I think it's safe to assume that this was not his first crucifixion as a Roman soldier. He had probably witnessed countless deaths, multiple times a week. Death was simply a part of his job, but something was different about this crucifixion. Something was different about this man named Jesus.

The Veil is Torn

From noon until 3:00, the whole earth is dark. Then, at 3:00 in the afternoon, Jesus cries out, "My God, my God, why have you forsaken me?" (Mark 15:34). With a loud shout, Jesus breathes his last breath, and the curtain of the Temple is torn in two from top to bottom.

The curtain (or veil) in the Temple is an important cloth that covered the Holy of Holies. This innermost place in the Temple was where the Ark of the Covenant was held. Only the high priest was allowed beyond the veil because it represented the separation of God's holiness from the sins of humankind.

Therefore, when this curtain is torn, it unveils God's amazing and powerful presence to humanity. As the retired Bishop Will Willimon says:

> *The Heavens, the curtain separating us from God, the veil in the temple that separates God's earthly dwelling from the world, is now wide open. High Priests, mediators between God and the world who worked that exclusive sacred space in the Holy of Holies, are no*

*longer essential for bringing us to God. God is present
with God's people here, now.*[50]

When that veil is torn, God's presence is literally
revealed to the centurion standing at the foot of the cross.
The Roman soldier's eyes are opened, and he sees Jesus
for who he truly is, the Son of God.

The centurion offers a powerful testimony right in
front of his fellow soldiers. Right in front of the crowds,
in front of all the other people standing around, he says,
"Truly this man was God's Son!" (Mark 15:39). It's
remarkable that a soldier responsible for carrying out
Jesus' death on the cross makes this powerful
proclamation about Jesus' identity as the Son of God!

The Green Mile

One of my favorite movies is *The Green Mile*, which is
originally a novel written by Stephen King. It tells the
story of a man named John Coffey who is large and
muscular. He towers above everyone else around him. He
seems very intimidating at first, but as you get to know
him you find that he is actually a gentle giant with a
loving heart.

Sadly, John has been sentenced to death after being
convicted of a crime that he didn't commit. The story is
set in the 1930's, and we find that John is a poor black
man who hasn't received much of any education.

John quickly wins over Paul Edgecomb (played by Tom
Hanks) and the other officers at the Cold Mountain
Penitentiary. It's not long before John begins to
demonstrate supernatural powers by curing Paul
Edgecomb's bladder infection, bringing a mouse name

Mr. Jingles back to life, and healing a dying woman named Melinda Moores.

They realize that there is more to John than meets the eye. They realize that John Coffey is an innocent man. Toward the end of the movie, Paul, has a discussion with John right before John is to be executed.

Paul: *"On the day of my judgment, when I stand before God, and He asks me why did I kill one of his true miracles, what am I going to say? That it was my job? My job?"*

John: *"You tell God the Father it was a kindness. I know you hurting and worrying, I can feel it on you, but you ought to quit on it now. Because I want it over and done. I do. I'm tired, boss. Tired of being on the road, lonely as a sparrow in the rain. Tired of not ever having me a buddy to be with, or someone to tell me where we are coming from or going to, or why. Mostly I'm tired of people being ugly to each other. I'm tired of all the pain I feel and hear in the world every day. There's too much of it. It's like pieces of glass in my head all the time. Can you understand?*

Paul: *"Yes, John. I think I can."*[51]

Paul ends up carrying out his duties, and John Coffey is put to death. It is a powerful and heartbreaking story.

There are a lot of comparisons between the Green Mile and the Gospel of Mark. For example, Jesus Christ and John Coffey both perform amazing miracles. They both take on people's burdens. They are both innocent. They are both put to death by capital punishment. They even have the same initials "J. C."

In fact, I can picture Jesus saying some of the same things as John Coffey, "I want it over and done. I'm tired of being on the road, lonely as a sparrow in the rain. I'm tired of people being ugly to each other. I'm tired of all the pain I feel and hear in the world every day."

Then you've got Paul Edgecomb and the centurion. They are both executioners. They both are responsible for carrying out capital punishment. They both recognize the innocence of the people that they put to death. They both recognize that there is something special about these individuals. They both recognize how God has worked through these men that are being killed.

I can imagine the soldier feeling similar to the way Paul Edgecomb felt. I'm sure he felt guilt and grief about being responsible for killing the Son of God. I'm sure the centurion thought, "What am I going to say to God on Judgment Day? I was only doing my job?"

But I'm reminded of something Jesus said while he was still on the cross, "Father, forgive them; for they do not know what they are doing" (Luke 23:34). Perhaps this statement from Jesus was a way for this centurion to accept Jesus' offer of forgiveness in his own life. Perhaps he was able to feel his heart changed. Perhaps he was able to go forward a changed man.

Transformation

The transformation of the centurion reminds us that God can change and transform our hearts as well. In fact, God is good at doing that. God does it all the time. God can take our hardened hearts and completely transform us.

158

The centurion in this story offers us hope. We are not defined by the worst things that we have done. The veil has been torn, and we are invited to experience God's presence and to accept God's forgiveness into our lives. We can be changed and transformed through the power of the Holy Spirit.

Prayer

Jesus, we remember how you suffered and died on the cross so that we could be at one with God. As we think of the Roman centurion in this story and how he witnessed and actively participated in Jesus' death, we are reminded of the guilt and shame and pain that he must have felt when he came to the realization that Jesus is indeed the Son of God. We know that we have betrayed Christ with our words and with our actions, but we also know that your forgiving love is offered to us. May we accept that forgiveness, be transformed, and grow as your disciples as we spread your love and share your word. For we ask all these things in Jesus' name. Amen.

Reflection Questions

1. While Jesus is hanging on the cross, he cries out, "My God, my God, why have you forsaken me?" Have you ever experienced a time in your life when you felt like God had abandoned you? Does it help knowing that Jesus experienced this on the cross?

2. Jesus teaches us about what it means to be forsaken. Who are the forsaken in our world? Who in our society is being overlooked?

3. After Jesus' death, a centurion proclaims, "Truly this man was God's Son!" Why do you think God uses unlikely characters? What does this tell us about the way God might be working in our world today?

4. We see a change occur in the Roman centurion. How might the season of Lent be a time for you to pursue transformation in your own life?

5. After Jesus dies, the curtain of the Temple was torn in two from top to bottom. What might the torn veil tell us about how our relationship with God changed because of Jesus? Do you think God is more accessible and present because of what Jesus did on the cross?

~

CHAPTER TEN

JESUS
IS RESURRECTED

When the Sabbath was over, Mary Magdalene and Mary the mother of James and Salome bought spices, so that they might go and anoint him. And very early on the first day of the week, when the sun had risen, they went to the tomb. They had been saying to one another, "Who will roll away the stone for us from the entrance to the tomb?" When they looked up, they saw that the stone, which was very large, had already been rolled back. As they entered the tomb, they saw a young man dressed in a white robe sitting on the right side, and they were alarmed. But he said to them, "Do not be alarmed; you are looking for Jesus of Nazareth, who was crucified. He has been raised; he is not here. Look, there is the place they laid him. But go, tell his disciples and Peter that he is going ahead of you to Galilee; there you will see him, just as he told you." So they went out and fled from the tomb, for terror and amazement had seized them, and they said nothing to anyone, for they were afraid.

(Mark 16:1-8)

One of the most meaningful services that I have ever experienced is a special service called, "The Sisters Speak: A Service of Scripture and Prayer." During the service several women from the community read various stories of silenced women in the Bible. We heard from women like Hagar, the daughter of Jephthah, the Unnamed Concubine, and Tamar. The service brought attention to some of the darker stories of how women have been mistreated, abused, and oppressed in the Bible. This service also brought attention to how women are mistreated, abused, and oppressed in our world still to this day.

The Role of Women

I think we often overlook the role that women play in Bible, especially in the story of Jesus. But the truth is, women play a crucial role in the life and ministry of Jesus. After all, Jesus was born of a woman, the Virgin Mary, who carried Jesus in her womb. She brought him into the world. She loved him, cared for him, and raised him. She was his mother, and he was her child.

In his adult life, Jesus had several interactions with women throughout the four Gospels. Numerous women are healed by Jesus, and there are numerous women serving Jesus. Jesus heals Peter's mother-in-law from a fever, and then she immediately starts serving Jesus (Mark 1:29-31). Jesus also heals a hemorrhaging woman (Mark 5:25-34). He raises a twelve-year-old girl back to life (Mark 5:21-43). He heals a woman bent over in pain (Luke 13:10-17). He witnesses to Mary and Martha and brings their brother Lazarus back to life (John 11:38-44). Jesus saves a woman who committed adultery from being stoned to death (John 8:1-11).

Jesus is consistently interacting with women during his life and ministry here on earth. In fact, women are the first to witness Jesus' resurrection. They are the first to see the empty tomb, and they are the first to tell others about Jesus being raised from the dead. The women are at the center of the resurrection story, but they are also at the center of the crucifixion story. In the Gospel of Mark, we are told:

> *There were also women looking on from a distance; among them were Mary Magdalene, and Mary the mother of James the younger and of Joses, and Salome. These used to follow him and provided for him when he was in Galilee; and there were many other women who had come up with him to Jerusalem.*
>
> *(Mark 15:40-41)*

Mark's Gospel waits until the second to last chapter to mention one very important detail. He waits until the second to last chapter to mention this important detail. It's almost like Mark includes it as an afterthought. He tells us, "Oh, by the way, the women were not only present at Jesus' crucifixion, but they have been present in Jesus' story all along." As Amy-Jill Levine says in her book *Witness at the Cross,*

> *The women had been with Jesus the entire time, from his days in Galilee to his final week in Jerusalem. Thanks, Mark; better late than never. Now when we read Mark again, we see the women at the healings, the teachings, and the controversies. They were there the entire time.*[52]

It's interesting that Mark shifts his focus to the women at this point in the story. Why now? Up until this point, the Gospels are primarily focused on Jesus' male disciples. There are numerous stories all about Simon Peter, Andrew, James, and John; However, at the cross and at the tomb – at the time when it matters the most – the women disciples are present, and the male disciples (other than maybe John) are nowhere to be seen. The male disciples have run away, they are in hiding. But the female disciples are right there next to Jesus throughout his entire journey to the cross.

The Women at the Cross

Mark mentions three specific women: Mary Magdalene, Mary the mother of James, and Salome. They are there as witnesses to the crucifixion. John's Gospel places the women (along with the disciple John) right at the foot of the cross; However, in Mark's Gospel, the women are standing from a distance. They are completely powerless and unable to stop the crucifixion from happening. They have no speaking parts, but their presence says it all.

The fact that they are even there in the first place shows their incredible strength and courage. The fact that they can even watch as a person that they love is tortured is remarkable. I can't imagine what they were feeling and experiencing as they watched on in horror as Jesus is being crucified on the cross.

Furthermore, being present during the crucifixion must also be very dangerous for them as well. They are risking a lot just by being there. They are risking their own lives. Their presence at the cross is a testament to their love and dedication to Jesus.

The women don't stop there, because they go on to risk their lives again after Jesus' death. These three women are the same three who go to attend to Jesus' body after his death. They go to anoint Jesus' body for burial after he has been killed.

The Women at the Tomb

The women in this story don't have enough time before the Sabbath to properly anoint Jesus' body for burial at the time of his death. Things have happened so quickly, and they simply run out of time. Now, they must wait 24 hours until they can go back and prepare his body in a ritualistic burial.

I don't image any of the three women get any sleep over the next 24 hours during the Sabbath. I'm sure they all stayed awake, crying, grieving, consoling one another; playing over the events from this past week in their mind repeatedly.

At the first opportunity, early on Sunday morning, Mary Magdalene, Mary the mother of James, and Salome go to Jesus' tomb. They bring the spices that they had prepared with them. Together, this group of women go to Jesus' tomb. There are no men with them. Again, the male disciples are nowhere to be found. They have scattered. The men are in hiding, but the women are the ones who have the courage go and to pay tribute to Jesus. They are the ones who have the determination to say goodbye to Jesus, to grieve the loss of Jesus, and to anoint the body of Jesus.

The women talk on their way to the tomb, and they wonder, "Who will roll away the stone for us from the entrance to the tomb?" (Mark 16:3). The stone that covered the grave was likely very heavy, and it would have been a real obstacle for them to move it. This big heavy stone might keep them out and hold them back from doing what they came to do.

The Gospel of Matthew tells us that Pontius Pilate orders for the tomb to be secured and even appoints soldiers to guard the entrance (Matthew 27:65-66). The stone covering Jesus' tomb was an especially large stone because the Romans wanted to make sure that the body of Jesus would not be disturbed. The Romans wanted to make sure that none of his followers would attempt to remove his body.

The women are aware that they do not have the strength to remove this large stone without help. Even with that question on their minds, they don't let it slow them down. They continue to walk toward the burial site, hoping to find a way to anoint Jesus' body.

Imagine the women's shock and surprise when, in the dark, just before dawn, they arrived at the tomb and see that the stone which once blocked the door to Jesus' tomb has been rolled away. I'm sure their minds were racing through all the possibilities to try to explain this unusual scene before them. Had they come too late? Have the male disciples already come to anoint Jesus' body? Maybe Joseph of Arimathea heard that the women were coming, and so he had the stone rolled away so that the women could come and anoint Jesus? Or maybe, heaven forbid, graverobbers or enemies of Jesus came and stole or desecrated his body?

Their anxiety and fear only increase when they enter the tomb and find that Jesus' body is indeed gone. He is nowhere to be found. The women are confused and perplexed, thinking to themselves, "Who rolled the stone away? Where is Jesus' body? Where have they taken him?" Imagine what it might feel like to come upon a grave of a loved one who has mysteriously disappeared. Imagine the confusion and fear and anger that you might experience.

The three women feel a flash of emotions, but then they encounter something else quite unexpected. There in the dark sat a young man in a white robe. It is almost as if the young man was expecting them, waiting for them to show up. The women, however, are amazed as the young man says to them:

> *Don't be alarmed. You are looking for Jesus of Nazareth, who was crucified. He isn't here! He is risen from the dead! Look, this is where they laid his body. Now go and tell his disciples, including Peter, that Jesus is going ahead of you to Galilee. You will see him there, just as he told you before he died.*
>
> *(Mark 16:6-7)*

The women are told the good news that Jesus is not dead. Jesus is alive. Jesus has risen from the grave. The young man wastes no time and commissions them to go tell the other disciples to meet the resurrected Christ in Galilee. The women are told to go and share the good news, but that is not what the women do.

Frozen in Fear

Terror and amazement overcome the women. So much so, that they don't say anything to anyone. They are too afraid to do anything. One of the major themes in Mark's Gospel is one of fear. The disciples go and hide in fear. The women are unable to share the good news because they are afraid. As Will Willimon states:

> *In the music of Easter, you may hear joy, majesty, glory, praise, but I don't think you'll hear much fear. Maybe Mark wants us to think about the good news at Easter not only as joyful, majestic, and glorious but also as fearful.*[53]

The Easter account in the Gospel of Mark ends quite abruptly. This is not surprising for Mark. Mark is the oldest

Gospel, the first written. It is also the shortest Gospel. It's quick and to the point. The earliest manuscripts of Mark do not include verses 9-20 of the Easter story. Scholars believe that the original text just ends at verse eight. It ends with fear.

The shock and fear of the situation seems to take over for the first eyewitnesses. The hiding disciples are not the only ones in fear. The women fear as well. They have walked into the tomb expecting to see a dead body. They thought that Jesus' story had ended. They thought that their relationship with Jesus was over between them; But to their surprise, and to their great fear, they realize that this is not the end. This is just the beginning.

The women don't tell anyone about the empty tomb because they are too afraid. Fear has paralyzed them, but it has also changed them. From this moment, the women realize that the world has been changed forever. They know that things will never be the same. They just don't know what to do with that knowledge yet, but we know that they will figure it out.

The women probably began to process what they had just experienced. They most likely think to themselves, "What if what the young man said is true? What if Jesus really has been raised from the dead? This can only mean one thing, God is on the move, God has let loose, and Jesus is alive."

You would think that the women would accept this truth and be eager to share the good news, but their fear gets in the way. Perhaps the biggest part of their fear comes from the realization that Jesus is indeed alive. If Jesus is in fact alive, then how might Jesus respond when he gets ahold of them? How angry will Jesus be with Peter and the other disciples? What will Jesus say to them? How can they face Jesus after failing to save him from the cross?

Not What We Deserve

Thank goodness Jesus isn't vindictive. Thank goodness Jesus doesn't gloat. Thank goodness Jesus does not seek retribution with his followers. If he did, we certainly couldn't blame him. After all, these are the people that he trusted the most, and these are the very people who betrayed him, denied him, and abandoned him. I'm amazed at how Jesus returns to these same people who were living in fear and anxiety. He returns to these ordinary people who have failed him over, and over again.

Notice that the resurrected Jesus doesn't go to the Temple in Jerusalem and stand before the chief priest and religious leaders to prove them wrong. He doesn't say, "See, I told you that if you destroyed this Temple, I would raise it up again in three days."

He doesn't travel to the palace of Pontius Pilate to haunt him and prove what a big mistake he had made. He doesn't go to Rome and confront Caesar and try to claim the throne for himself. Jesus doesn't offer any, "I told you so's." Jesus doesn't gloat. He doesn't say, "I'm right and you are wrong!" He doesn't do any of that.

Instead, Jesus makes a habit of presenting himself to the lowly. A handful of times, after his resurrection, Jesus appears to the most ordinary people you can imagine. He appears to none other than his very own disciples. For whatever reason, Jesus sees more value in appearing to those former fishermen and female disciples, than he does to the powerful rulers and leaders of his day.

Thank goodness that God doesn't give us what we deserve. We don't deserve forgiveness. We don't deserve grace. We have done nothing to deserve God's love. But Jesus went to the cross anyway, for you and for me. In this act of sacrificial love, Jesus offers us grace when we really deserve damnation.

In the end, it was God's divine love that moved God to send us Jesus. It was Jesus who was lifted up on the cross, and on Easter we celebrate how Jesus was lifted up again. We remember the palms, the passion, and the resurrection.

Mary in the Garden

In John's Gospel, Mary Magdalene is the first to experience the Risen Christ. Mary is at the tomb, and she is completely distraught. The hopelessness that Mary faces in this moment is something that we all face at times. In those dark moments of life, we are left wondering, "Will I ever get through this? Will things work out? Is everything really going to be, okay? Is there any hope?" Miraculously, it is during this dark and difficult moment when Mary experiences the Risen Christ.

Jesus, disguised as gardener, sees Mary crying and asks her, "Woman, why are you weeping? Whom are you looking for?" (John 20:15a). At this point, Mary still thinks that someone has stolen Jesus' body. She responds, "Sir, if you have carried him away, tell me where you have laid him, and I will take him away" (John 20:15b).

Jesus calls out her name, and she instantly recognizes him. Her whole attitude changes in that very instant. She is no longer in despair, she is no longer without hope, because she has experienced the resurrected Christ.

What happens next is interesting. Mary is so used to having Jesus around, and she thinks that he is back for good. She thinks things will go back to the way they used to be and so she grabs ahold of him. When she touches him, Jesus responds:

> *"Do not touch me, because I have not yet ascended to the Father. But go to my brothers and say to them, 'I am ascending to my Father and your Father, to my God and your God.'"*

> *(John 20:17)*

The resurrected Christ is alive. He is on the move, and he's got things to do. Like Mary, we don't always realize that. We think Jesus just lived a long time ago, but we forget that he is still very much alive today. Jesus died and rose 2,000 years ago, and this act is still changing the course of human history. He is alive and is among us, and he is just waiting for us to experience him as the resurrected Christ.

Mary goes forth and shares the good news that Christ is risen! Christ is risen indeed! This is the first sermon after the resurrection of Jesus, and it is delivered by a woman. She witnesses the resurrected Christ, she believes in him, and she shares the good news.

The Commission

In the additional, longer, ending of Mark, the Risen Jesus returns to his followers and commissions them to proclaim the good news and make new disciples. Jesus says:

> *"Go into all the world and proclaim the good news to the whole creation. The one who believes and is baptized will*

be saved, but the one who does not believe will be condemned. And these signs will accompany those who believe: by using my name they will cast out demons; they will speak in new tongues; they will pick up snakes, and if they drink any deadly thing, it will not hurt them; they will lay their hands on the sick, and they will recover."

(Mark 14:15-18)

The story of Easter is a reminder that Jesus is still willing to work with people like you and me to do God's work in the world. Despite our confusion, despite our fear, despite our disbelief, God calls us to go out and make disciples. God calls us to go out and love one another. God calls us to experience the Risen Christ moving and working in our world and in our lives today.

In the Resurrection, we catch a glimpse of a new world that suddenly becomes visible. We catch a glimpse of a world where peace and justice prevail. The beautiful thing about Easter Sunday is that it reminds us that we serve a Risen Savior. We serve a God who is alive. We serve a God who moves and works in and around our lives each and every day. Because of the Resurrection, nothing in this world has ever been the same since. May we encounter the Risen Savior!

Prayer

God of the Resurrection, you have entered this place. You have come to disrupt our way of life. Allow us to experience the Resurrection in our own lives today. May we be like the women who remained faithful and followed you through your journey to death and new life. May we find ways to experience your grace and love as we do the things you have called us to do. May we go out and share your good news with the world. May we experience the Risen Christ, and may we be transformed through your love. For we ask all these things in Jesus' name. Amen.

Reflection Questions

1. The women go to the tomb early in the morning to prepare Jesus' body for burial, but they were surprised to find the tomb empty. How has God surprised you in your own life?

2. In the empty tomb, the women encounter a young man who tells them that Jesus is alive, but the women were seized with fear. Has fear ever prevented you from doing something God has called you to do?

3. After Jesus' resurrection, he isn't vindictive toward the people who have harmed him. How might you embrace God's grace and forgiveness instead of revenge and vindication in your own life?

4. Because of the resurrection of Jesus Christ, the world will never be the same. How does the resurrection story change the way that you live your life?

5. After the resurrected Jesus appears to his disciples, he commissions them to go and share the good news and make disciples. How might you live into that call to make disciples?

ABOUT THE AUTHOR

Rev. Andrew Curtis Lay is an ordained elder in the United Methodist Church and is currently serving as the pastor at Wesley Memorial and Carlock United Methodist Churches in Etowah, Tennessee. He has also taught as an adjunct professor in the religion department at Tennessee Wesleyan University. He is the author of an Advent book entitled: *Hope for the Holidays: Exploring the Message of Hope in the Christmas story.*

Hope for the Holidays

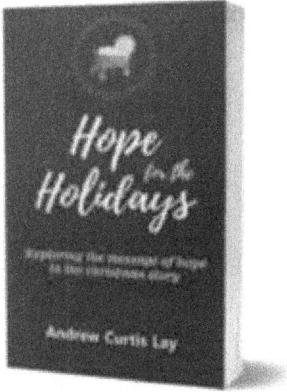

Hope for the Holidays is more than just a catchy phrase that you might find in a Hallmark greeting. Hope is vital to our lives, and it is often the most prevalent during the season of Christmas. This book speaks about the message of hope that we find in the Christmas story as we celebrate Jesus' birth. In this book, we will look at the different characters in the Christmas story and how they offer a message of hope to us in our own lives.

ISBN: 1637460287

Kharis Publishing

For more information about Andrew Lay, visit
https://www.andrewcurtislay.com

NOTES

1. Unless otherwise noted, all Scripture is taken from New Revised Standard Version.

2. Eugene M. Boring, *Mark: A Commentary* (Louisville, KY: Presbyterian Publishing Corp, 2006), 252-253.

3. Paula Fredriksen, "When Jesus Celebrated Passover," *The Wall Street Journal* (Dow Jones & Company, April 19, 2019), last modified April 19, 2019, accessed February 3, 2021, https://www.wsj.com/articles/when-jesus-celebrated-passover-11555685683.

4. Thomas G. Long, "Palm Sunday (Mark 11:1-11)," *The Christian Century*, last modified April 4, 2006, accessed February 22, 2021, https://www.christiancentury.org/article/2006-04/rhetorical-excess.

5. Amy-Jill Levine, *Entering the Passion of Jesus: A Beginner's Guide to Holy Week* (Nashville, TN: Abingdon, 2018), 25.

6. William H. Willimon, *Collected Sermons of William H. Willimon* (Louisville, KY: Westminster John Knox Press, 2010).

7. See Genesis 3:19.

8. *The Faith We Sing: Pew Edition* (Nashville, TN: Abingdon Press, 2000), 2138.

9. "Jerusalem Timeline," *Ancient History Encyclopedia* (Ancient History Encyclopedia, n.d.), https://www.ancient.eu/timeline/jerusalem/.

10. Jan Nylund, "Court of the Gentiles." In J. D. Barry, D. Bomar, D. R. Brown, R. Klippenstein, D. Mangum, C. Sinclair Wolcott, & W. Widder (Eds.), (The Lexham Bible Dictionary Lexham Press/Logos, 2016).

11. Amy-Jill Levine, *Entering the Passion of Jesus: A Beginner's Guide to Holy Week* (Nashville, TN: Abingdon, 2018), 50.

12. Leander E. Keck, *The New Interpreter's Bible Commentary* (Nashville, TN: Abingdon Press, 2015), 501.

13. William Hulitt Gloer, *Feasting on the Word: Preaching the Revised Common Lectionary, Year B, Volume 2: Lent Through Eastertide*, ed. David L. Bartlett and Barbara Brown Taylor, (Louisville, KY: Westminster John Knox Press, 2008), 95.

14. Martin B. Copenhaver, *Jesus Is the Question: The 307 Questions Jesus Asked and the 3 He Answered* (Nashville, TN: Abingdon Press, 2014), xviii.

15. John Wesley, *The Sermons of John Wesley: A Collection for the Christian Journey*, ed. Kenneth J. Collins and Jason E. Vickers, (Nashville, TN: Abingdon Press, 2013), 302.

16. Cynthia A. Jarvis, *Feasting on the Word: Preaching the Revised Common Lectionary, Year B, Volume 4: Season After Pentecost 2*, ed. David L. Bartlett and Barbara Brown Taylor, (Louisville, KY: Westminster John Knox Press, 2009), 238.

17. Martin Luther King and Coretta Scott King, *Strength to Love* (Boston, MA: Beacon Press, 2019).

18. William L. Holladay, *A Concise Hebrew and Aramaic Lexicon of the Old Testament: Based upon the Lexical Work of Ludwig Koehler and Walter Baumgartner* (Grand Rapids, MI: Eerdmans, 1985), 218.

19. "Smoke and Mirrors," *The Crown,* season 1, episode 5, (2016) *Netflix.*

20. Frederick W. Danker, and Walter Bauer, editors. *A Greek-English Lexicon of the New Testament and Other Early Christian Literature.* Third ed., (University of Chicago Press, 2000) 661.

21. "The Origin of the Word 'Companion'," *Merriam-Webster* (Merriam-Webster, n.d.), accessed August 24, 2021, https://www.merriam-webster.com/words-at-play/history-of-word-companion.

22. Andrew Foster Connors. *Feasting on the Gospels – Matthew, Volume 2: A Feasting on the Word Commentary*, ed. Cynthia A. Jarvis and E. Elizabeth Johnson, (Louisville, KY: Westminster John Knox Press, 2013), 8.

23. William Shakespeare, *Julius Caesar, William Shakespeare, Act 3, Scene 1* (New York, NY: Spark Publishing, 2014).

24. Nancy A. Mikoski, *Feasting on the Word: Preaching the Revised Common Lectionary, Year A, Volume 2: Lent Through Eastertide*, ed. David L. Bartlett and Barbara Brown Taylor, (Louisville, KY: Westminster John Knox Press, 2010), 238.

25. Anne Horton, Mark Earey, and Perron Gay, *Understanding Worship* (London: Bloomsbury Publishing, 2001), 76.

26. John Wesley, *The Sermons of John Wesley: A Collection for the Christian Journey*, ed. Kenneth J. Collins and Jason E. Vickers, (Nashville, TN: Abingdon Press, 2013), 86.

27. *The United Methodist Hymnal Book of United Methodist Worship* (Nashville, TN: The United Methodist Publishing House, 2001), 14.

28. Paraphrase of "Confession and Pardon" in the United Methodist Hymnal, 12.

29. Strong's NT Lexicon 1068: Γεθσημανῆ.

30. "Hematidrosis (Sweating Blood): Symptoms, Causes, Treatment," *WebMD* (WebMD, n.d.), accessed November 10, 2022, https://www.webmd.com/a-to-z-guides/hematidrosis-hematohidrosis.

31. *The United Methodist Hymnal Book of United Methodist Worship* (Nashville, TN: The United Methodist Publishing House, 2001), 607.

32. Dennis F. Kinlaw, *Malchus' Ear and Other Sermons*, Cricket Albertson (Wilmore, KY: Francis Asbury Press, 2017), 37.

33. Harper Lee, *To Kill a Mockingbird* (New York, NY: HarperCollins, 2002), 201.

34. Talmage Boston, "Who Was Atticus Finch," *Texas Bar Journal* 73, no. 6 (June 2010): 484-485, accessed December 1, 2021.

35. Douglas O. Linder, "The Trials of 'The Scottsboro Boys,'" Famous Trials. University of Missouri-Kansas City. (December 2016), accessed January 28, 2017.

36. Ibid.

37. Bryan Stevenson, *Just Mercy: A Story of Justice and Redemption* (New York, NY: Spiegel & Grau, 2015), 17.

38. Stanley Hauerwas, *Hannah's Child: A Theologian's Memoir* (Grand Rapids, MI: William B. Eerdmans Pub. Co., 2012), 231.

39. "Antonia Fortress," *Madain Project*, accessed December 31, 2021,https://web.archive.org/web/20200529204714/https://madainproject.com/antonia_fortress.

40. Marcus J. Borg and John Dominic Crossan, *The Last Week: What the Gospels Really Teach about Jesus's Final Days in Jerusalem* (New York, NY: HarperCollins, 2006), 143.

41. See: Matthew 27:15-22.

42. *Hotel Rwanda*, 2004.

43. *The United Methodist Hymnal Book of United Methodist Worship* (Nashville, TN: The United Methodist Publishing House, 2001), 62.

44. Fred B. Craddock, *The Collected Sermons of Fred B. Craddock* (Louisville, KY: Westminster John Knox Press, 2011), 102.

45. Audrey West, *Feasting on the Word: Year A, Volume 2* (Louisville, KY: Westminster John Knox Press, 2010), 181.

46. Dietrich Bonhoeffer, *The Cost of Discipleship* (New York, NY: Touchstone, 2018).

47. Ira Glass, producer. "Kid Logic." Transcript. In *This American Life*. Public Radio International. June 22, 2001

48. Thomas à Kempis, *The Imitation of Christ* (Milwaukee, WI: Bruce Pub. Co., 1940), 71.

49. *The Book of Discipline of the United Methodist Church 2016* (Nashville, TN: United Methodist Publishing House, 2017), ¶ 104. p. 74.

50. William H. Willimon, "Truly, God's Son," *Pulpit Resource* Vol. 49, No. 1, Year B, (March 28, 2021).

51. Frank Darabont and Stephen King. *The Green Mile*. Burbank, CA.: Warner Brothers, 1999.

52. Amy-Jill Levine, *Witness at the Cross: A Beginner's Guide to Holy Friday* (Nashville, TN: Abingdon Press, 2021), 89.

53. William H. Willimon, *Will Willimon's Lectionary Sermon Resource: Year B, Part 1* (Nashville, TN: Abingdon Press, 2017), 253.

www.ingramcontent.com/pod-product-compliance
Lightning Source LLC
Chambersburg PA
CBHW072039080426

42733CB00010B/1942